Jan Brokken was born in 1949 in Leiden. He studied at the School of Journalism in Utrecht and took Political Studies at the University of Bordeaux. He is one of Holland's most highly regarded writers. He has published novels and short stories as well as travel narratives and literary journalism. His passion for travel influences his fiction and non-fiction alike. His previously published books translated into English include *The Rainbird* (Lonely Planet, 1997), of which Elisabeth King in the *Sydney Morning Herald* (3rd May 1997) wrote, 'This is travel writing at its most enthralling, meaningful and engaging.' *Jungle Rudy* is currently being made into a film.

Sam Garrett has translated many Dutch authors including Tim Krabbé, Arnon Grunberg, Karl Glastra van Loon, Nanne Tepper, Lieve Joris, J.M.A. Biesheuvel and Dirk Draulans. He was given an honorable mention in the Vondel Prize 1999 and was the winner of the Vondel Prize in 2003 for his translation of *The Rider* by Tim Krabbé. He lives in France and Amsterdam.

GW00391446

JUNGLE RUDY

Jan Brokken

translated from the Dutch by
Sam Garrett

MARION BOYARS
LONDON • NEW YORK

Published in Great Britain and the United States in 2004 by
MARION BOYARS PUBLISHERS LTD
24 Lacy Road, London SW15 1NL

www.marionboyars.co.uk

Distributed in Australia and New Zealand by Peribo Pty Ltd
58 Beaumont Road, Kuring-gai, NSW 2080

First published in Holland in 1999 by Atlas as *Jungle Rudy*.

10 9 8 7 6 5 4 3 2 1

A CIP catagolue for this book is available from the British Library
A CIP catalog record for this book is available from the Library of Congress

 The publishers would like to thank, and acknowledge the financial support
of the Foundation for the Production and Translation of Dutch Literature.

 The publishers would also like to thank the Arts Council of England
for assistance with the translation of this book.

ISBN 0-7145-3103-0

Set in Bembo 11/14
Printed in the UK by Bookmarque, London

Contents

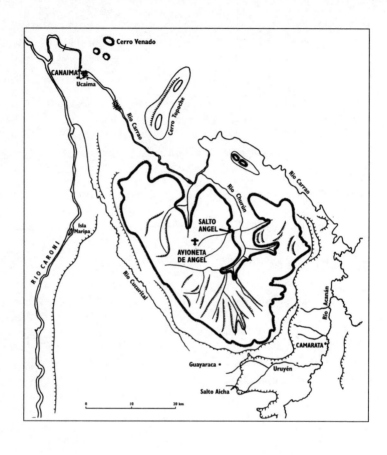

Truffino and Dunsterville's map of the area around
Canaima and the Auyán Tepui

I

In His Lost World

He wasn't waiting for me when I got off the plane at Canaima. At least, I didn't see a man I should have recognized immediately by his ears: the right one had had a chunk bitten out of it by a rattlesnake while he was sleeping in his hammock, floored by the midday heat; the top of his left lobe had been gnarled by leishmanianis, a disease carried by a parasite of the sand flea, which goes with the rainforest the way seasickness goes with the sea. There was an Indian, however, leaning on the fence that showed where the landing strip stopped and the savanna began, an Indian with floppy ears. There were also a couple of women dressed against mosquito infestation and wearing so much khaki that at first I mistook them for soldiers. But the man I was looking for wasn't there, a man in his sixties who rarely shaved, whose hollow cheeks and emaciated body were reminders of the times he'd had visions of banquets while he himself dined on ants.

One week earlier I had sent him a fax with an urgent request to accompany me to Angel Falls. Even with a big outboard on the back of the *curiare*, it would take a day or two to motor up to those falls, and if what I had heard was true, he could easily talk our way through all those long hours on the river. Besides that, he could do so in my mother tongue. For though his name didn't immediately show it, Rudy Truffino had been born in the Netherlands, in The Hague.

His amazing career and his tattered ears, his restless eyes and his rattling laugh had been described to me by several friends on Curaçao, during the years that I had lived on that island. They had made long journeys with him into the area he had opened up with the help of the Pemón Indians, an area that spread out below the Orinoco, an area the size of the Netherlands; they had planted the seed of amazement in me by telling me that he spoke the language of the Pemón, shared their aversion to property, and seemed to get along better with those semi-nomads than with his former compatriots.

What endeared him to me immediately was that his way of coping with the wilderness was to listen regularly to *Don Giovanni*, or to a very old recording of Ella Fitzgerald, or to a trumpeter whose soulful notes he could imitate perfectly as he washed the sweat from his body with river water after a difficult trek. In the middle of nowhere he had also surrounded himself with thousands of books, which was not difficult for me to imagine – I would do the same, deep in the jungle. That he had spent the last years of his life with an Indian woman gave me the feeling that he careened back and forth between two worlds; I have a weakness for people like that.

Truffino's wife had died and his three daughters had moved to the city, but he had stayed on in the Gran Sabana. What he'd told my friends in Curaçao was that he wanted to be buried in the jungle, not in a cemetery; cemeteries were too crowded for him, and he had become pretty much used to the wide open spaces.

So he continued to guide the lovers of unspoiled nature up wild rivers to the tallest waterfall in the world. He didn't even ask much for his services; after a long, dry period on Curaçao, I had sent him a fax.

Not that I was planning to write about him – I had just

finished a novel and meant to spend my weeks in Venezuela thinking quietly about the next one – but I already saw him as a man of novelistic character. I had run into Europeans in desolate areas before who had gone off in search of the unknown, out of distaste for a life predictable as a book of hours, and I had been impressed by them, because I had never entirely succeeded in severing the bonds with my own past. Between leaving your country for an extended period and disappearing lies half a world of difference; they were not only born vagabonds, they had left never to return again, and what always intrigued me was how they had arrived at that decision, and whether they never regretted it. 'The good traveller,' says a Chinese proverb, 'knows where he is going; the perfect traveller forgets where he came from.' But I was not convinced that one could achieve perfection in that regard. Truffino, of course, thought differently; one of the things I wanted to ask him on our way upriver to the waterfall was how he had overcome the fear that always kept me on the straight and narrow – the fear of not belonging anywhere. He didn't seem like the kind of man who would answer that with a shrug; besides, a trip on a lonesome river like that inclines one to plain speaking.

Confident that Truffino would mention their names often, I had read before I left the classic travelogues by Von Humboldt, Bates, Wallace, Spruce and the Brothers Schomburgk, who had navigated the rivers surrounding the Gran Sabana, and those by Koch-Grünberg and Im Thurn, who had entered the area first without being able to penetrate it too deeply. I read the novels by Conan Doyle, Gallegos and Carpentier, set against the background of the high mesas, Thomas's study of the Pemón Indians, reports by Ruth Robertson about the first major expedition to Angel Falls, and the bundle of newspaper and magazine articles that Millicent Smeets-Muskus had given me when I told her I hoped to travel with Rudy Truffino. Millicent had interviewed him in 1984 for the Curaçaoan daily *Amigoe*, and she was conscientious enough to have saved a box file full of all her documentation on Truffino and the Gran Sabana.

From Carácas I flew to Cíudad Bolivar, the town founded by the Great Liberator on the mucky banks of the Orinoco, from Cíudad Bolivar to Canaima. The plane was a Boeing, but it buzzed the canyons like a Cessna, granting me a glimpse of Angel Falls: two narrow streams that fell from a colossal mesa and landed hundreds of metres below at the top of a densely wooded valley. Through the window of the little plane I saw a few other mesas looming faintly on the horizon, four or five of the ninety-four that lie in southeastern Venezuela, northern Brazil and in the Cooperative Republic of Guyana, formerly British Guiana. In the language of the Pemón Indians, the mountains are called '*tepuis*' or '*tepuys*', 'houses of God', but from the air they look more like islands surrounded by a sea of cloud. Others have noted the resemblance as well, albeit in a different way: the geologist Uwe George, whose *National Geographic* article I had spread on my lap, spoke of these mesas as 'islands in time'.

The *tepuis* are the remnants of the Guyana Shield, the oldest sandstone formation in the world, dating from the time when Africa and South America were still one. Some of them are five, six, seven hundred kilometres in circumference, most of them are more than two thousand metres high. Because of their complete isolation, ninety-eight percent of the plants that grow atop them are found nowhere else in the world, plants from before the Deluge, plants – and perhaps animals and insects as well – that have elsewhere died out or evolved in a completely different fashion in the time it took Africa and South America to drift apart. Or, as Carpentier puts it: 'Plants that fled from man in the beginning, to hide themselves away, here in the last valleys of prehistory.'

When Rudy Truffino came to the Gran Sabana in the 1950s, almost nothing was known about the area; in terms of scientific exploration, it was as untouched as the moon.

As the plane started its approach, I saw the spot where Truffino had built his first camp, an incredibly beautiful place right across from five waterfalls that tumbled over red rocks into a lake. The second camp he built with his bare hands is located a few kilometres to the south, along the banks of the Río Carrao. He had named the first camp '*Canaima*', the word the Pemón Indians use to refer to the spirit of evil. Evil, according to the Pemón, almost always comes from far away, from the top of a mountain, from a neighbouring tribe in search of conflict, or from strangers blinded in their quest for jewels and gold. When the Pemón saw their first white men, it seems they whispered '*canaima*', and ever since Rómulo Gallegos used that word as the title for his novel about the unknown southeast of the country, it has become a household word in Venezuela. Truffino named his second camp '*Ucaima*'. It lies close to a waterfall that continues to rush even during the dry season: '*ucaima*' means 'that which draws all to itself'.

The Indian with the floppy ears jumped over the fence and introduced himself. His name was Josef Gregori and, as it turned out, he worked at Rudy Truffino's camp. That very same day he told me that his father had been born in northern Italy, and that his mother came from the Gran Sabana. From his Indian mother he must have inherited his small size and the straight, blue-black hair cut in bangs across his forehead:

the hairstyle of the old Caribes, who cut their locks with the razor-sharp jaws from the dried head of a piranha. Two things I then found out about his father: that he had named him Josef – a possible indication of Tyrolean ancestry – and that, not long afterwards, he had left and never come back.

Josef took me to the river in his truck, along a road which the rain had turned into a muddy creek. Before putting my baggage in the *curiare*, he first had to bail the rainwater out of the big dugout with a tin can: my suitcase and backpack he covered with a plastic sheet.

Veils of rain whipped across the river as we made our way up to the camp. The rainy season had arrived in full force; within the space of a single day, the river had risen a metre. We passed an Indian village; I hunched down deeper inside the plastic raincoat that protected me from the rain and the wind. A steady wind was blowing, in the middle of the river it was downright cold, not what I'd expected in an area only six degrees north of the equator. But a few minutes later, when I stepped out of the *curiare* and Josef handed me my suitcase, it was warm again.

Crossing a grassy field, I passed beneath a tree which Josef said had been planted after the earthquake of 1967. It looked as though it had been there for centuries. Right behind the tree was the hub of the camp, a building with the curved walls of an Indian hut.

'*Señor Rudy*,' Josef said as we walked past a photograph on the wall – Truffino, wearing a felt hat, a long-stemmed pipe clenched between his teeth. It was unmistakable: the portrait was by a professional photographer, his quarry that self-confident expression on Truffino's face.

'*Y señora Gerti.*'

Truffino's wife was holding a toucan by the feet; behind

her, three little blonde girls were dancing on a bench of bamboo slats, and on Rudy's knee was an *acure*, the largest of all marmots.

On the same wall with the photo hung spears, baskets, bows and arrows, blowguns and other Pemón artifacts that Truffino had collected through the years, not so much to build a collection, but to keep them from being thrown away, and to keep people from forgetting how the Pemón had lived before the Gran Sabana was opened up.

After I was seated at the table, Josef served me lunch. I was the only guest. In the distance I heard a man talking on the phone in rapid Spanish; I had also seen two chambermaids, small Indian girls, who disappeared around a corner as soon as they saw me; there had to be a cook somewhere, too, but the only person who showed his face during lunch was Josef. I did receive a visit from an animal with a long snout, round ears and brown, bristly fur with light grey stripes through it. A tapir. When Truffino had found it in the jungle, Josef told me, the tapir was so little it could barely stand on its own legs; now it weighed at least a hundred kilos.

It stopped raining. While I inhaled the aroma of the strong Venezuelan coffee Josef served me after lunch, butterflies the size of handkerchiefs went fluttering past; these were the impressive *morphos*, with wingspans of up to twenty centimetres, metallic blue wings that catch the light with every movement and reflect it in a dazzling glow.

The sun broke through, the temperature skyrocketed. Josef suggested we take the boat up to Salto Sapo, one of seven waterfalls close to Canaima; I asked him whether it wouldn't be better for me to talk to señor Rudy first about our trip to Angel Falls, but Josef said we'd see to that later; at this time of year, one needed to seize every dry moment.

As we climbed into the boat, the sky turned a blue that rivalled the blue of the butterflies. It was less than half an hour to Sapo; to get as close as we could to the falls, however, we would have to walk some distance through the jungle.

We had barely crossed the first hill when Josef bent down to examine the purple fruit of a plant. He zipped open his hip pouch and took out a little paper sack: I was to hold the sack open for him while he pressed the seeds out of the fruit. When one had an infected eye, he gave me to understand, the best thing was to put a couple of these seeds under your eyelid and keep them there for the night, so they could absorb the dirt that was causing the infection. About fifty metres further along he plucked a few young leaves from a mango tree; if you let them steep in boiling water for half a day, the infusion would heal any infection. Coming down the hill he pulled a few shoots off a liana-like vine; the *bejuco decadena* is by far the best remedy for diarrhoea. And when we were almost at the bottom, he took some leaves from the *hoja anestesia*; if you chewed them when you had a toothache, the pain would be gone within fifteen minutes. His next find, the fruit of the merey, the cashew, he praised as the best of all remedies for a sore throat; at the bottom of the hill he scraped some sap off a tree trunk; a very good cure for bronchitis.

As a child, his grandmother had taught him which leaves belonged to which trees; later she taught him what you could do with those leaves. Josef had grown up in Cíudad Bolivar, the city on the broad, brown river where his mother had gone to try her luck. He was about six when his grandmother came to live with them. His Italian father had disappeared years before, his mother worked at a laundry; it was his Indian grandmother who raised him. Once he had grown up, he was curious to find out where all her knowledge had come from, and he was the only one of her grandchildren to return to the Gran Sabana. He had worked in the kitchen at the camp at Canaima until señor Rudy hired him as a guide. It was señor Rudy who had completed his education; he turned out to be as knowledgeable about nature as Josef's grandmother, and what he didn't know he could look up in his library.

When we arrived at Sapo, Josef reached out and took my hand. He led me under the falls; the rock formed a roof above the path, we could sidle our way along behind the curtain of water, but one false step meant a fall of fifteen or twenty metres.

Through the veils of water I could see a mesa on the horizon, square as a block, reddish-brown and robust, a temple towering over the savanna. The foot of that temple was choked with trees and bushes; around the roof, dark clouds were swirling, as though a hurricane had broken loose up there.

To get in before the rain, we headed back to the boat. At the bottom of the hill we met up with an Indian family. In the reed basket the father carried over his shoulder I saw rolled-up hammocks, a rolled-up mosquito net, a machete, a large knife, a rifle. The children weren't carrying anything; in her basket the mother had pots and pans, a plastic dishpan and a couple of plastic bowls. These nomads' entire household could have weighed no more than fifteen kilos. There were on their way to the next *conuco*, where they would stay for a few months, or for a few years, depending on the quality of the soil. Most of the soil in the Gran Sabana is arid, not really fit for agriculture, and after three or four years even the best fields produce almost nothing. The plots of land the Pemón cultivate are very far apart as well, which keeps them moving all the time.

We got into the boat; the man, woman and children crossed the river barefooted, jumping from one boulder to the next, and walked off into the savanna.

'*Etamen waki*,' Josef shouted after then, which turned out to be the standard farewell among the Pemón. Literally, it means: 'Have a nice walk.'

We took the *curiare* up the Rio Carrao. There was thunder in the distance; the Auyán Tepui was hidden by rain clouds, but through them we could see the bolts of lightning. It was late afternoon by the time the sun broke through again, and then it was the savannas – where only tall grass and the occasional moriche palm grew – that were swathed in mist.

'The Lost World' is what Sir Arthur Conan Doyle called this remote corner of Venezuela. He never visited the area himself; Doyle wrote his science fiction novel after attending a series of lectures in London by the botanist Everard Im Thurn. 'The unknown bears in from all sides,' he wrote in *The Lost World*, which appeared in 1912. 'What lies outside the narrow passageways of river? No one knows.'

In 1884 Everard Im Thurn had climbed the Roraima, one of the easternmost *tepuis*, and he had reached that mesa by trekking in a wide circle around the Gran Sabana, by way of British Guiana. Back in London he showed his audiences an amazing number of plants that had never before found their way into a botanical specimen box, and that set Conan Doyle's imagination rolling; in *The Lost World* he described not so much a lost world, but a hidden one, a world that hovered between heaven and earth and had remained beyond mankind's ken for hundreds of thousands of years.

In the *tepuis* there are holes which are sometimes three hundred metres deep and eight hundred metres wide. In 1964, the English bush pilot Harry Gibson was daring enough to fly low over the Sarisariñama and let his plane dip down into one of those holes. During that mortally dangerous dive, he saw only thick undergrowth all the way to the deepest depths of the crevice, thereby leaving unanswered the question of what lurked beneath that dark green mass.

Dinosaurs, Sir Conan Doyle suspected when he wrote *The Lost World*, and ape-men who had escaped the draw of evolution. The Pemón believe in something similar; they say that atop the Sarisariñama lives a gigantic beast that comes down off the mountain at night and eats people, and while it eats it makes a smacking sound very like '*sari sari*'.

In the early 17th century, Sir Walter Raleigh must have picked up something of that legend; he reported that, in the area south of the Orinoco, there lived a tribe of men whose heads were lower than their shoulders, who had one eye in the middle of their chest and giant, fan-shaped feet which they used as an umbrella.

Dangling on a rope let down from a helicopter, Charles Brewer-Carías descended into one of the holes in the Sarisariñama – the thick vegetation made it impossible for the helicopter itself to land. He found no cyclopes, but he did find a great number of previously unknown plants. He couldn't penetrate far into the chasm, but what he saw of the caves there led him to believe that they were the remnant of what had once been an extensive system of underground rivers. It was, without a doubt, a mysterious world up there, and I was curious to hear about Truffino's experiences.

After dinner that evening, Josef left for Canaima. Before climbing into the *curiare*, he set two cans of beer beside my chair and handed me a couple of scrapbooks, to wile away the hours.

'Don't forget: señor Armando turns off the generator at eleven,' he warned me before leaving. 'When he does that, you won't be able to see your hand in front of your face. So go to your room a little earlier and light the candles; they're beside your bed.'

Señor Armando, I supposed, was one of the two men who had been sitting at the bar when we came back from Sapo Falls. The little stocky one, perhaps, who seemed to be making a leap into space every time he climbed down off his barstool. Or the heavier man who, between gulps of whisky, had chewed on the the little gold necklace that he had slid up over his chin. They'd both mumbled '*hola*', without looking at me.

Truffino apparently wasn't at the camp; but then he'd be bound to show up tomorrow or the next day. Meanwhile, Josef would guide me around the area; he was a nice man who knew a lot and saw the humour in a great many things, so I didn't object.

I leafed through the scrapbooks. There were four of them, the fifth having been eaten by the tapir. Four books containing newspaper and magazine articles, interviews and travel stories and photo series from Venezuelan, American, English, German and Dutch publications. Some of the articles I recognized from Millicent Smith's documentation; others added new facts to the long series of setbacks that comprised Truffino's life. I sat there and read all evening, the only sound to distract me that of the flitting of bats' wings; the next morning I made my first entries in the little notebook I always carry with me, just in case.

Truffino had been straining at the bit to leave Holland almost before the war was over. In interviews he had never talked about what made him so keen about that self-exile: in fact, he said very little at all about his youth. Sometimes he joked that his father had been an ice-cream vendor, and that he'd had little desire to follow in his footsteps and spend his whole life shouting '*gelato, gelatino*'; other journalists were told that it had not been easy to leave, and it had ultimately taken him seven years before he could truly begin a new life on this side of the ocean.

The first place he'd tried was Africa. Space was the thing he found most important about a place, and whether that space consisted of desert or savanna made little difference to him; he would have to prove himself on either desert or savanna, and he was young enough at the time to still see that as something heroic.

He had worked on a stock farm on what the Tunisians call the Low Steppes, an area regularly flogged by sandstorms. A huge plain, with little clumps of grass here and there that would only grow if watered on a daily basis, but the water never came; the government failed to meet its contractual duties, and the cattle died. Truffino lived in a barracks, the place he slept enjoyed the hygienic standards of a latrine; when he got up in the morning, he was lucky to have even a few drops of water come out of the tap. Typhoid fever and malaria put an early end to his stay in Tunisia; for weeks, he had teetered on the brink of death.

Once he had gained a little strength, he took a bus to the capital, dragged himself down to the harbor and used his last bit of money to buy a ticket for the ferry to Marseille. During the crossing, the fever returned; he slept through the entire trip, awoke only when most of the passengers had already disembarked, and discovered that his final belongings had been stolen.

Back in Holland he attended classes in veterinary medicine for a while, until he saw an ad in an English newspaper asking for a *veterinario* on one of the biggest islands in the Antilles. He didn't really think it would work out, but when his letter received a positive reply, he never hesitated for a moment. He hopped on a plane for the Dominican Republic, was taken on at the presidential palace, and from then on bore the title of esquiry to General Trujillo. The job involved little more than currying the dictator's horses and occasionally helping his children into the saddle.

He had just started speaking a bit of Spanish when mutinous soldiers forced their way into the palace. He waved his Dutch passport vehemently, but was still arrested; in the truck that took him away the next morning he heard about the coup against Trujillo, and that all of the dictator's accomplices were to be executed. At that moment, General Trujillo was in New York, lobbying for the Dominican Republic's admission to the United Nations.

Truffino didn't have to think about it long. At the next curve, he jumped out of the truck. He heard the crack of rifles behind him, but he was lucky, he had landed in a ditch and the bullets went zinging over his head.

Outside the presidential palace he knew only one man, a horse-lover who also happened to be the ambassador of Venezuela. That evening the diplomat smuggled him aboard a ship that left the next day for La Guiara; Truffino hid himself beneath a tarp and crossed the Caribbean as a stowaway.

In Carácas he slept under bridges and viaducts, and sold cookies on street corners.

Thanks to its oil, Venezuela had been transformed within a few decades from a backward farming state to the richest country in South America. With the petrodollars, immigrants also came flowing into the country. Carácas had numbered no more than five hundred thousand souls in the early 1950s, but had since grown to a city of millions; the military regime of General Pérez Jiménez did its best to attract as many Europeans to the capital as possible, in order to throw up the apartment buildings, offices and hotels at an even faster pace. They arrived by the thousand at the port of La Guaira: Spaniards, Italians, Germans, Americans, and Dutchmen as well – around four thousand in the years 1951 to 1954 alone.

Truffino scraped together most of his revenues around the Tamanaco. With six hundred rooms, the hotel would, upon completion, be the biggest in Carácas; five restaurants, a nightclub, shops, swimming pools and a dining terrace that looked out over the entire valley, a city within a city. Truffino sold his cookies not only to the construction workers, but also to the hotel's first staff members. One of the managers, who couldn't place his accent, asked where he came from and whether he spoke any other languages. One week later Truffino was working at the desk; one year later he was appointed night manager.

At the bar of the Hotel Tamanaco he met Charlie Baughan,

a meeting that was to be a turning point in his life. On the first page of Truffino's scrapbooks was a picture, not of himself or his family or his camps, but of the man who flew him into another world, and paid for it with his life.

Charles Baughan, an experienced bush-pilot who flew mostly for TACA Airlines ('*Terribles Accidentes Cada Año*' was the joke in Carácas), had an office on the ground floor of the new hotel, and drove everyone crazy with his stories about the Gran Sabana. At first Truffino only listened, then he learned to fly, with Baughan as his instructor. After the lessons they made plans together, at Baughan's home, in the neighbourhood called San Bernardino, amid the spare plane parts, the bows and arrows, the blowpipes and other Indian relics the American had collected on countless journeys into the interior.

From a distance, one would have said that Baughan had the build of Orson Welles and the face of Ernest Hemingway. But those who came closer were shocked by the flattened nose and the battlefield of scars beneath the jaw line. The rare few who saw him in the bush without a shirt on never dared to look too closely again: his skin was a mass of sutures and badly healed burns.

Baughan had started his career in Mexico, where he had learned both to fly and to shoot. He flew to areas where the *Guardia Civil* never showed its face, and usually had to maintain order around the landing strip himself, which earned him the nickname '*Pancho pistola*', 'The dummy with the pistol'. He may have looked like a bullfight aficionado, but Baughan was the kindest man in the world, and when things really got iffy he would start humming 'The Three Little Lambs'.

In the late 1930s he had heard a fellow bush-pilot in Panama tell tall tales about the mesas and savannas between the Orinoco and the Amazon. That pilot telling the stories had the smoky voice and puffy face of an Arizona bartender; the world's highest waterfall had been named after him, though, because he was the first to fly past it, and because, when he tried to put his plane down close to the head of the falls two years later, he had crashed there. And also, of course, because he had the right name for it: Angel.

On the mountain with the waterfall, Jimmy Angel said, there were millions of dollars worth of gold waiting to be found. Angel had done an awful lot of things in his life, so Baughan could hardly imagine that he was exaggerating. After all, a pilot who had flown straight through a German zeppelin in the First World War just to blow it up didn't really need to brag; and, in a certain sense, Jimmy Angel wasn't bragging either.

Baughan flew to Venezuela and secured the necessary permits. Then he flew to Santa Elena de Uairén, on the southeast side of the Gran Sabana, close to the Brazilian border. The settlement there had been established by Lucas Fernández Peña, and the diamond miner had built twenty-eight houses in less than fifteen years' time, and sired twenty-seven children.

At Santa Elena de Uairén, Baughan saw two emaciated miners collapse from hunger. He offered them a meal of fried eggs with bacon and beans, and the men unfolded a banana leaf to show him the diamonds they had found by the Icabarú Riber. A week later Baughan cleared a level area beside that same river; one month later he was flying to the Icabarú.

In exchange for gems or a gold nugget he brought the garimpeiros food, clothing and tools. He built huts at Icabarú, laid a street and brought in new diamond hunters by plane, thirty on each flight, sometimes as many as one hundred and fifty a week.

In 1942, when a 154.15-carat stone was found in a heap of rubble, the run on Icabarú really began. Baughan could have made a fortune many times over, if only he hadn't passed out crates full of medicine to the Indians; with the arrival of thousands of white men, the Pemón had contracted many illnesses against which they could produce no antibodies. In addition, on his flights back to Cíudad Bolívar Baughan regularly transported the badly injured – Indians or diamond hunters who had broken their back, shoulder or ankle in the rapids. He felt it was almost inappropriate to charge them for that, and he usually ended up paying for the surgeon and the hospital as well.

In late 1942 he entered the Canadian Royal Air Force, perhaps not completely voluntarily – he was still an American citizen, and the Allies had suffered such heavy losses that they were conscripting every experienced pilot they could find – or perhaps voluntarily, for Baughan was a dyed-in-the-wool democrat. In the mining town of Icabarú he had hoped to set up a daily newspaper, but his friends talked him out of it; they said the only thing the diamond hunters really longed for was a brothel. Baughan's counter argument was that a brothel would come of its own accord, something you couldn't say of a newspaper.

In the service of the Canadian RAF Baughan carried out hundreds of reconnaissance flights and bombing missions over Asia, the Middle East, Northern Africa and Europe. He was shot down three times, suffered burns all over his body, and ended his military career with the rank of colonel. But back in Venezuela, everyone just knew him as 'Charlie'.

By the time Rudy Truffino flew with him, Charlie Baughan knew the southern portion of the Gran Sabana like the back of his hand. And he was particularly interested in exploring those parts of the northern section that were indicated with a green spot on the official maps, areas where

26

the course of the rivers and streams had not yet been charted, and where, with the exception of the occasional gold seeker, no one from the civilized world had ever set foot.

Whenever they had a few days off, they would fly from Carácas to the savannas south of the Orinoco. To pay for the flights, they occasionally took with them a wealthy guest from the Tamanaco who was willing to pay a few hundred dollars to catch a glimpse of an area that could not be reached overland, and to which all written accounts ascribed a disquieting beauty.

'A place where the riverbed dances in the glimmer of golden light and beautiful fish catch the glistening in their scales,' Sir Walter Raleigh had reported in the early 17th century. Like so many explorers, he had come no further than the beginning of the Rio Caroni, where a gigantic waterfall blocked his way, falls that made the noise of 'a thousand great bells being struck together'.

The Pan-American Highway, which now runs along the eastern edge of the Gran Sabana, was completed only in 1973, after the army had been called in to blow up the hard layers of sandstone. The immense savanna could not be reached by water; there are dozens of rivers wandering through the area, but they are not all connected, and most of them are so dangerous that the Indians first blur their childrens' vision with eyedrops of a tincture of tobacco or pepper before committing their dug-outs to the waterfalls and rapids.

Baughan and Truffino followed that part of the Rio Carrao downstream of the waterfall discovered by Jimmy Angel in 1935. On one of his flights, Baughan had seen another waterfall, not an exceptionally high one like Salto Angel, but broad. At five spots he had seen the water roaring down along red rock into a lake, whose elongated form and banks of crystal-white sand reminded him of a lagoon. The water of that lake was of the same deep red colour as the rocks on the bottom, and that must have given Baughan and Truffino the idea of naming the spot Canaima, which in addition to 'spirit of evil' also means 'blood feud'. At one end of the lake the water fell again, and then Río Caroni followed its course.

Baughan set his plane down on a reasonably level patch of ground, close to rapids which the Indians called 'Mayupa'. Close to the sandy banks of what he persistently called 'the lagoon', he had built a couple of huts. From the Mayupa to the lagoon, however, was a five kilometre walk, partly over land and partly through the river, which made provisioning difficult and the bringing in of heavier equipment and building materials impossible.

He and Truffino found another spot where a plane could land, this time much closer to the lagoon. They cut down the trees and bushes there and levelled the ground to make an airstrip; every time they returned, however, they first had to buzz the high grass in order to chase away the wild animals.

Baughan and Truffino's interest was at first prompted by the promise of gold and precious stones – ever since Jimmy Angel had taken off from the Auyán Tepui with seventy pounds of gold nuggets, every bush-pilot had become a gold-digger – but gradually they developed a much better plan. At Hotel Tamanaco they had heard about an upcoming expedition that the New York Botanical Garden was planning, another expedition organized by the Instituto Botánico in Carácas, the Chicago Museum of Natural History's expedition, and a German one as well, organized by the University of Göttingen. Close to the lagoon they could set up a base camp; Truffino could guide the scientists through the jungle on trips that would easily take two or three weeks, and Baughan could arrange for transportation between Canaima and the capital.

They organized junkets from Carácas for potential investors. A German businessman was interested in putting money into the scheme, and so was his sister. The third participant was a Dutchman who had sold his hotel in Paramaribo, in the belief that Venezuela was the new land of opportunity.

In January of 1956, Charlie Baughan brought Truffino back to the lagoon, so he could explore the area further and establish contact with the Indians. From the air they had sighted five or six settlements, and Baughan was convinced they should undertake nothing without permission from the *capitanes*, the chiefs of the Pemón. Two weeks later he would come back to pick up Truffino.

Baughan, who was approaching fifty, had brought his young wife along. On the trunks of the trees along the northern shore of the long lake, Mary Baughan had casually pointed out fifteen different varieties of orchids. When she saw one of the orchids in full bloom, she could no longer keep to herself what she had been thinking all along: everything they did here was bound to succeed.

They chose the spot where they would build the camp: it was to be right across from the waterfalls. They swam in the blood-red water of the lagoon, they let the sun dry them on the powdery sand, they felt the first bites of the sand fleas. When the sun was no longer so fierce, Baughan and Truffino lifted the chest of supplies out of the plane and carried it to the storeroom: six poles in the ground with a roof of palm leaves on top. In the distance they heard the dull pounding of a thunderstorm, a pounding that echoed for a long time in the cañon between the mesas. 'Like after a bombardment,' Truffino recalled later.

As the last rays of sun were disappearing behind the mountains, the DC3 went lurching down the runway of grass and red dirt. It was Saturday, January 28th, 1956. Mary Baughan waved her white shawl out the window as the plane's wheels bounced over the last tussock of grass; just before the Dakota banked away from the line of hills across the lagoon, she let it fall. Rudy picked up the shawl and tied it around his neck.

Along with a photo in which he and Charlie Baughan are standing together in the high grass of the savanna, that white silk shawl was the only physical reminder of the Baughans he would ever have.

From Canaima Baughan flew to Maturín, a town close to the Orinoco delta, where he picked up seven passengers. Then he flew back to Carácas. Baughan did not receive clearance to land at Maiquetía airfield; the weather was too bad. He decided to try Higuerote, but never arrived; the fuel ran out, the plane crashed.

Fourteen days later Truffino was waiting for him at Canaima. He knew Charlie was a punctual man, and when the Dakota didn't appear he knew that Charlie had died at the controls. In the days that followed he came to understand the full extent of the unforgivable mistake he had made: he had informed no one in Carácas about where he was going. Except for Baughan and his wife, no one knew exactly where he was. It could take weeks, maybe even months, before a plane would land in this area again. The cans of rations were empty; he would have to fend for himself in a place where, as he had found out by now, the trees bore very little in the way of comestibles.

On the morning of the twenty-first day, an Indian came by, an old Indian on his way to fish further upriver. Truffino pointed to his bow and arrow, upon which the man, who wore only a loincloth made of bark, pointed to Rudy's clothes. He didn't have much choice: better to go through life naked than hungry. In exchange for his shirt, his trousers and his shoes, he received the bow and arrow and a bit of curare in which to dip the arrows.

The next day the Indian came by again, and taught Truffino how the Pemón bid each other farewell: with the same words Josef would teach me thirty-nine years later.

'*Etamen waki.*'

'Have a nice walk.'

The next morning Josef didn't show up. In the middle of the afternoon, as he finally stepped out of the *curiare*, he taught me a new word in Pemón: '*mumba*', meaning 'hangover'. And he added another word as well: '*mumba kaypun*', which means 'bad hangover'. Not that he had drunk so much himself; it was the boatsman who had disappeared into the jungle with two bottles of rum, and at first light was still nowhere to be found. It had taken Josef all morning to locate him.

Under the gigantic tamarind along the river I leafed on through the scrapbooks, saw the occasional dugout come gliding by, a motionless oarsman at the helm, a motionless oarsman at the prow, for the current was strong enough here to push the boat along by itself. I let the silence sink in. At nightfall the jungle on the other shore must come alive, at early light it must sound like a aviary, but around noon the sounds died out and the quietness was from before the dawn of creation.

The next morning Josef and the sobered-up boatsman took me to Canaima; from there Josef drove me to the airstrip in a truck.

The newest among the flying crates along the strip must have been thirty years old; the bush-pilots were bidding against each other for passengers, like Arab merchants. The minimum number of passengers for the DC3, the same kind of plane in which Charlie Baughan had brought diamond hunters to Icabarú and in which he had crashed in the mountains above Higuerote, was reached within an hour. There are still dozens of those Dakotas plying the skies of Venezuela; Avensa has two that fly out of Canaima, to bring tourists past Angel Falls.

Right after take-off, through the big square window of the Dakota, I saw the same thing Baughan and Truffino must have seen forty years earlier from the cockpit; the lagoon with the sandy white beach on the right, five waterfalls in the middle and, to the left, falls number six and seven. On the other side of the lagoon, the river left a black trail through vast woods and savannas where the grass was more yellow than green. In the distance two mesas were dimly visible, and behind them and to one side the Auyán Tepui stretched out, a country unto itself.

'When I saw that,' Truffino told a reporter from *The Miami Herald* in 1965, 'I was ready to leave everything behind, right away. That was the moment when I received my 'call of the wild'.

In a book about the discovery of America, which I later found in his library, Truffino had underlined the following sentences from Columbus' journal: 'This is the finest, most lovely country in the world. [...] There are pines, oaks, aloe and palms, but much more verdant than in our country or in African Guinea. [...] Here you have beautiful rivers, excellent water, gardens and pastures, and you see lovely songbirds in such numbers that they sometimes block out the sun.'

'Canaima,1955,' Truffino had written in the margin.

The Dakota was piloted by two veterans. I was able to get a good look at them, because they hadn't bothered to close the cockpit door behind them. Both men wore khaki uniforms, both of them looked like cattle breeders from the *llanos.* I asked the older of the two whether he had know Baughan, whereupon he spoke a sentence in English (albeit with a strong Spanish accent) that I felt like writing down right away.

'Listen, buddy, when Death comes early, he usually takes the wrong person.'

Baughan, as I heard, was a scatterbrain who started all kinds of projects without ever really getting anything off the ground; if he hadn't met Truffino, Canaima would never have been more than a couple of huts. But sloppy as he was on the ground, he was a master of precision in the air; he never took an unnecessary risk. Most other pilots were complete or partial idiots, driven mad by alcohol, driven to alcohol by fear. With their far-too-light and usually badly serviced single-props, it was always a gamble for them to fly between the mesas; the air pockets there not only made the planes drop like a brick, but the wind in the canyons was wild and unpredictable as well, and many a plane had been blown against a mountain. Pilots who are scared often try to prove differently by pulling stunts, but Baughan had flown over every sea, every ocean, every continent, and most of his hours at the stick had been wartime hours; he didn't need to prove a thing. In a plane, therefore, he was a model of caution.

'And he, of all people, had to crash because of his own stupid mistake. Because he took just a little less fuel than he really needed. It's not fair, is it?'

The pilot shook his head, and the plane banked to the left.

The DC3 had followed the river, then the valley of the Río Churún. Now we were approaching the Auyán Tepui and heading into clouds. The pilots' real work was about to begin; I hurried back to my seat.

There are almost always clouds hanging above and around

the Auyán Tepui; that morning, however, there were sizeable holes in those clouds. When we flew into one of them, I saw a wall coming up that must have been at least two thousand metres high. The plane shimmied, rocked, dipped way down, giving me a better view of the rock wall, which was yellow in some spots, brownish-red in others, and a greyish-black elsewhere. Between those somber tints one saw an occasional mysterious glimmer of white light. Right at the bottom of the wall the trees crowded together in a forest that was more often brown than green, but between those autumnal colours there was sometimes a tree in purple, or bright orange.

We came closer to the mountain, the wings looked like they were scraping rock. I braced myself, the way you do in a car that suddenly brakes with squealing tyres; at that same moment the plane banked off sharply and I saw Angel Falls, close by: two narrow streams plummeting almost a full kilometre, between 979 and 1030 metres according to the most recent measurements, nine hundred of which were in a complete free fall.

Below, the water vanished into the forest's rimples. The sun shone like a spotlight through the clouds and turned the narrow stream into a luminescent trail; from the air it looked like a burning fuse wending its way through the brownish-green mass.

The plane dove into clouds again. It turned away from the mountain, came around full circle and flew past the waterfall again, this time a little lower. The water looked like it was splashing on the right wing.

Then the Dakota nosed up out of the valley, so sharply that my knees were pulled up towards my neck. The plane thumped and shook and made a deafening noise. The clouds parted; the flat mountaintop was beneath us.

For five or ten minutes we flew over bare, stubborn rocks with deep chasms between them, and here and there a swampy area with mossy vegetation.

'*Señor.*'

The oldest of the two pilots pointed to the fold-down chair in the cockpit.

I sat down behind him.

'There...that's where Jimmy Angel crashed in 1937.'

His finger tapped against the big square side-window of the cockpit.

Two minutes later.

'There...'

The wreck of a helicopter.

'There...'

The wreck of a Cessna.

'There...'

He said it with a resigned smile.

'For flyers like us, the Gran Sabana is the big cemetery. But without flyers, the Gran Sabana would not yet be on the map.'

Rudy Truffino fed himself with ants, and with worms, the most disgusting things a person can put in his mouth. He had traded in his clothes for a bow and arrow, but it takes years of training to shoot a fish in the river and bring it to the surface. He didn't even bother with wild animals; he would have been torn to pieces before he'd even pulled back the bow.

He was twenty-seven years old, and not entirely convinced that he would ever reach twenty-eight. Under normal conditions he was already only skin and bones; after a month at Canaima, the bones began showing through the skin on his arms and legs.

A snake bit him on his big toe. He wiped away the blood and saw two purple dots: the bite of a bushmaster, along with the *fer-de-lans,* the biggest viper on earth and the most venomous. He took his knife, made two cuts in his toe and squeezed out the venom, then walked up the hill as slowly as he could, without exerting himself. He lay down in his hammock and told himself that, if he hoped to stay alive, he must not move a finger. When he woke up the next day, his leg was swollen. He didn't budge; if he tried to sit up, the venom would spread further through his body. He had to remain lying down, which was easier said than done; the snakebite brought on a burning thirst, his throat began feeling like the desert that once almost cost him his life in Tunisia as well, a thirst that became even worse once the fever and the vomiting started. But he did not get up and stumble to the lagoon for a drink. He remained lying like that for three days, for three days he hallucinated about water, for three days his foot felt like a chunk of stone. On the fourth day, he could move his leg again.

Years later he read a scientific report that proved him right: of the hundred people who died as a result of a snakebite, ninety-five died of shock, and not from the venom. Some people even died from the bite of a snake that wasn't even venomous. Years later, that is what he would tell others as well: as long as you stay calm, you'll be okay, even when logic seems to say you're going to die. But of course, one must also be capable of calm when one's foot turns blue, then purple, then takes on a gangrenous sheen.

The days without food or water had weakened him even further. The worms and the big flying leaf-cutting ants he stuffed in his mouth did not do much to bolster his condition. When the old Indian came by again, he walked past a dying man. The next day he stopped, took a good look at the white man and made a suggestion.

'Let's walk.'

They walked to the north, through an area Truffino knew only from the air. Three hours later they arrived at a *conuco*.

The old man spoke to his daughter, a woman in her forties who scratched at her bare breasts as she listened to her father speak. The white man's arrival didn't seem to surprise her at all. The closest mission post was more than a hundred kilometres from the plantation, and she couldn't have seen very many white people in her life, but she greeted Truffino as though he were just one of the Europeans who came by every week, ladled some reddish juice out of a calabash and gestured to him to drink it.

The *cachiri* was full of fibers, and so bitter that he had to swallow three times after each sip he took. But the juice, brewed from the root of the yucca, quenched his thirst and made him a little drunk, so that he lost his fear and reacted a little less drowsily.

He bowed his head to the woman, asked her in Spanish what her name was.

'Lola.'

Far from the civilized world, he was talking to a woman named Lola. The Capuchin monks had done their work well; every Indian they baptized was required to adopt a Christian name, and by 'Christian' the monks from Madrid and Seville meant Spanish.

'Lola...what?'

'Lola Castro.'

He whistled in amazement and she led him to a stool in front of the hut. He barely had time to sit down before she'd pressed a flat biscuit in his hand. He sniffed at it, and thought he recognized the smell of manioc. He was to use the biscuit to dip up meat from a pot on the fire. He hadn't eaten meat in weeks, and wondered whether his taste buds were still working well; besides the meat, he also tasted fish. He took a second bite, and a third; then a bone pricked his tongue. It was fish, after all; both meat and fish in the same pot.

At the next bite, he choked. There were at least ten different varieties of peppers in the pot. His throat burned, but at the same time he felt that Death had taken a step back and was no longer eyeing him so emphatically.

He looked into Lola Castro's eyes and, when she nodded, a great peace came over him. Her father offered him a hammock in the big oval hut; he stretched his legs, and from the other hammocks a young man and a young woman and seven or eight children nodded at him as well. None of the faces seemed to reflect even the slightest suspicion.

Later he understood that the Pemóns' entire world of thought revolved around *canaima*. It was no coincidence that their language used the same word for both 'vengeance' and 'evil'; the spirit of evil manifested itself in the form of a person who was out for revenge. The Pemón believe, however, that they can deflect *canaima* by offering the stranger a bowl of *cachiri*, by presenting him with tender meat, by leaving him satisfied. And if they also succeed in drawing the stranger into their own circle, the *canaima* is completely averted. A pragmatic system of belief, in other words, cautious and cheerful at the same time; on the one hand the stranger brings misfortune, on the other it can be prevented by a hospitable welcome.

It was a little community in which Truffino found himself. Even in the biggest Pemón *conucos* there are never more than ten or eleven families. The *conucos* are spread far apart as well; David John Thomas, who carried out the first thoroughgoing study of the Pemón in 1982, calculated that there was one settlement, with an average of five or six families, per one hundred square kilometres. He estimated the total number of Pemón at five thousand, thereby giving an implicit explanation for why they don't become aggressive when someone enters their territory: they have enough space as it is. The Venezuelan government gave a higher estimate; officially, there are eleven thousand Pemón living in the Gran Sabana. But even if that estimate was correct, it still amounted to no more than the occasional soul in an area of forty-thousand square kilometres.

'If we live too close together,' the Pemón told Truffino, 'the fighting starts.' So they kept enough distance between them to rule out conflicts. Aggressive behaviour was punished by banishment; a man who started a fight was no longer allowed to take part in the hunt, and was given no more *cachiri*, so that his teeth soon chattered with fever. The Pemón regard *cachiri* – which is actually extremely rich in vitamins – as a source of strength.

Truffino was completely accepted into the little Indian community. He learned the Pemón language, he learned their customs. He learned how to bring fish to the surface by sprinkling *barbasco*, a poisonous tree bark that leaves the fish gasping for oxygen, into a slow-moving part of the river; he learned how to shoot with one of the old-fashioned Brazilian breechloaders the Pemón used to hunt tapir and deer and the lightning-fast *tigre* which in most other Indian languages is known as the *ja-gu-ar*, 'he-who-kills-at-a-pounce'; he learned to use the bow and arrow and the blowgun with which the Indians hunted smaller game, primarily *lapa* (capybara) and agouti. The *chiquïri*, a large semi-aquatic rodent, they killed with the spear, as they did the clumsy *oso palmera*, the giant anteater, whose razor-sharp digging claws could be very dangerous.

The Pemón often returned empty handed from their day-long hunting expeditions. Koch-Grünberg, the first ethnologist to come in contact with the Indians of the savanna, noted as early as 1911 that the Waika (the name by which the Pemón were known until the 1960s) were, of necessity, 'near-vegetarians'. Like the humans, wild animals on the Gran Sabana were also permanently in search of food, and the enormous distances they crossed made them hard to locate. Furthermore, most of the game stuck close to the mesas, a place where the Pemón were afraid to set foot.

At first Truffino couldn't understand why the *tepuis* were off-limits to the Pemón, and why the Auyán Tepui in particular provoked in them a visible fear. Not only they did they never set foot on the mountain, they also never canoed *around* the mountain. They actually considered it a mortal risk to even look at the mountain; that was why they always stayed dozens of kilometres away from the mesa.

The literal meaning of *auyán* gave him a bit of an inkling; *auyán* means biggest, greatest or most powerful; the gorge between the Auyán Tepui and the neighbouring Wei Tepui is called Devil's Canyon; the Auyán is also referred to *Montaña del Infierno*. Nevertheless, Truffino kept trying to figure out what was so hellish about that mountain.

It was its shape, Lola Castro told him, the shape of a house.

A bond of trust soon developed between him and Lola. She taught him Pemón, word by word, corrected his pronunciation, and when he was able to start asking questions she told him about the whole gamut of fears that dictates life in the wilderness. It was a sign of bravery on her part, for the Pemón do not like to talk about the spirit world, and especially not to outsiders.

To the Pemón, the Auyán Tepui is the home of the *mawari*, spectres who resemble humans and spend their days singing and dancing. The luminescent white spots on the rock walls are the windows of their house; from there the mawari keep an eye on the savanna. The mawari steal the souls of the living, and cause illnesses. The shaman can sometimes track down the spectres by chewing on certain leaves and entering a trance, but if he comes back empty-handed from his trip through the spectral world, the illness will run its course.

Every faith is based on fear, and the closer he came to the mountain the better Truffino could home in on the source of that fear. In the narrow canyon around the Auyán Tepui the cold air falling off the mountain collides with the warm air of the savanna; thunderstorms are frequent there, and the reverberations of the thunderclaps unleash pandemonium in the valley. The lightning bolts flashing across the river kept the Pemón away from the infernal mountain; as a favourable side-effect, the Auyán Tepui, the biggest of the mesas, with a surface area of seven hundred and fifty square kilometres, had for centuries remained close to its primal state. There had never been any hunting, any fishing or any agriculture, not even in the surrounding area. This meant that no stretches of forest had ever been slashed and burned to build *conucos*. Truffino could safely assume that he was the first man to ever set foot in the thick forest around the mountain.

Along with Lola Castro's brother and son, he explored the Río Churún and its countless tributaries. How he had ever convinced the two Pemón men to go with him was one of the things I hoped to ask Truffino during our trip up to Angel Falls. It must have taken a great deal of *cachiri*, and a great deal of persuasive power. From everything I had read about him, Truffino seemed to be a charismatic man, quick to laugh and make others laugh as well. He exuded confidence as well; all those who travelled with him had the impression that he was fully in control, even as the boat smacked against rocks in the rapids. 'Out on the river,' I heard from one of my friends in Curaçao, 'he had the stoicism of a shaman.'

He made the very first trip all alone, but he couldn't get far without the help of the Castros; in those days the dugouts were not yet equipped with outboards, he had to paddle, and on the way out that meant bucking a strong current. Whenever he arrived at rapids, he had to pull the boat out of the water and drag it overland, which was almost impossible. But after he returned from his first trip in one piece, the Castros were no longer afraid to go with him, and when nothing happened to them either, their fear diminished a bit;

the mawari, it seemed, were not inclined to action when there was a white man around.

Overland, though, Truffino must have done a great deal of exploring on his own. The Auyán Tepui looks a lot like an impregnable fortress; according to the Indians, only one path led up, a path they never followed, but Truffino found a second one leading up from Ahonda Canyon on the north side.

Back at the *conuco*, Truffino stuffed some dried tobacco leaf in his pipe, lay down crosswise in his hammock and listened. He was continually amazed at how peaceful the Pemón were in their dealings with each other, and how they tried to avoid any conflict with outsiders; this was all the more striking when one realized they were descendants of the Caribes, the nomadic people who had moved from Brazil to the northeast in search of the fertile land where the sun rose. Their exodus had been a grim one (they had no qualms about sinking their teeth into a piece of human flesh), and was the kind of stuff of which myths are made: they were searching for the source of light, and therefore of all life. Ultimately, the Caribes reached the islands off the coast of the continent. During the centuries of migration, however, certain tribes followed other paths, like the Pemón, who found their destination in the Gran Sabana and soon lost their cannibalistic bent. The many expressions and concepts in their language that refer to the sea support the more recent hypothesis that the Pemón first migrated with the rest to the coast, and later returned to the Gran Sabana.

On the wide savannas between the mesas, the men turned to fishing and hunting while the women worked the fields. The harvesting was done together. The Pemón behaved as though they were out to make sure nothing remained that might remind one of the boisterous conquerors of yesteryear; screaming at another person was something they strongly disapproved of, and even raising one's voice was considered a sign of bad manners.

The way in which they lived together was the epitome of reasonableness. No one held power in the Pemón community; some people had influence, and that influence stemmed from knowledge. People listened to the shamans because they could drive out illnesses, and to the *taren esak*, the sorcerers, because they could summon up spirits. The *capitanes* had influence because they were able to resolve conflicts and allay feuds. Truffino gradually came to see that for which David John Thomas, in *Order without Government*, would provide the scientific support a quarter of a century later; among the Pemón, no one is an authority by reason of his function, but only because of what he has achieved or what he knows. Truffino himself earned the Indians' respect because he was able to stop people from bleeding, and because he could set broken arms and legs.

According to Thomas, Pemón society was egalitarian, anarchic (without any form of government; the chief was a negotiator, and nothing more) and, in a certain sense, inchoate, because many authority structures were missing. A Pemón had to decide for himself again and again about the borderline between the permissable and the forbidden, and respected that borderline out of fear of banishment or angry spirits.

The low authority-content among the Pemón manifested itself in all matters of etiquette. Truffino had to become accustomed to the fact that his Indian companions considered the giving of orders to be highly unbecoming. When he wanted to go upriver with the Castro men for a long journey, he could never say: 'Let's go.' He had to say: 'It is a full day's journey to the Rio Churún.' Upon which the Castros would say: 'Yes, then it is time for us to be going.' If they didn't say that, Truffino simply had to wait until they started getting ready: the slightest show of impatience had the adverse effect.

The main reason for the Pemón's peaceful behaviour was undoubtedly their lack of property. What someone used (a machete, a rifle) was part of his personal gear – when he was not using it, it had no owner. Land belonged to the tribe, not to anyone in particular, so conflicts were ruled out.

The same willingness to oblige applied to immaterial matters. The Pemón did not marry, they lived together; they knew no marriage rituals, in fact they had no word for 'marriage'. Girls were allowed to have coitus before finding a permanent partner; men considered being a virgin at seventeen more an indication of unattractiveness than of any virtue. A man could have more than one woman; a woman who was tired of her man could untie her hammock from the pole and move back in with one of her brothers, with no sanctions applied. The Pemón only became aware of their own nakedness when they saw white men wearing clothes; they regarded sex as the most normal thing in the world, and no one had to leave the hut to find it. The children's hammocks hung beside those of their parents, and children watched as their parents made love. Even that phrase is not entirely in keeping with their worldview; the hammock moved, and it moved more frequently when a woman was pregnant, for the Pemón see the foetus as a plant that needs to be watered regularly with sperm.

The word 'family' was also not part of the Pemón vocabulary; the word with which they expressed kinship was 'my place'. When a woman gave birth, she did so as quickly as possible, preferably standing in the river; the man, on the other hand, went and laid in the hammock for days, imitating the contractions and the moans of childbirth, to show that he was the father.

Another thing I hoped to ask Truffino was just how chastely he had behaved during those months. Had he ever crawled into the hammock with an Indian woman? He never talked about it later on. Perhaps Lola had warned him not to, or perhaps he didn't want to take the risk. Little was known about the Pemón in 1956 – Truffino may have heard from Baughan that they were the kindest people in the world, but Baughan had never spent months among them. Only in the course of time would he discover how mild and gentle they actually were. Polygamy does not rule out jealousy; when the men fought, it was usually over a woman. On the other hand, Truffino must also have known that the Capuchin friars almost invariably kept an Indian mistress, but perhaps that custom offended his own sense of honour. The Pemón had saved his life, and for that reason alone he would have done everything in his power not to violate the trust they placed in him.

What he appreciated most about the Indians, however, was their versatility. They were fishers and hunters, farmers and artisans. With the same ease with which they steered their boats through the rapids they built a settlement within a few weeks. For miles and miles around, they knew their way perfectly through the forest, across the savanna, over the rivers, and when they did lose their way they navigated by the moon and stars. Neither the vegetable kingdom nor the world of the spirits held any secrets for them; they knew the origins and significance of every ritual action. The Pemón never dreaded packing up their things and starting all over again at another location; they resigned themselves to their restless fate, and when anyone expressed wonder at their frugal existence, they were told: 'But we never suffer hunger.'

In all things, the Pemón remained a nomadic people. Why then should they need many possessions? The more they collected, the more they had to drag along once the soil was exhausted and the time had come to found a new *conuco*. They were not bound to the ground they lived on, or to their huts, which were made of wood and palm leaves and were often open on two sides, offering less shelter than a tent; and in those huts they kept almost nothing. Their life consisted of walking, boating and talking, and talking – hours, nights of talking – until the *cachiri* was finished and they had to make a new batch. The talking sometimes blended into singing, and the singing was a way to breathe new life into old legends. Early the next morning they sang again, to summon up the spirit of the jaguar, or some other animal whose tracks had been found nearby. Everything they did had a melody that went with it.

It was in the jungle that Truffino found the way of living that suited him best. He too was restless by nature, he too considered it a sign of great spiritual wealth when one was satisfied with little. None of which made the step he finally took any less drastic: by leaving the city behind, he went back thousands of years in time.

He came from a world that was quickly becoming Americanized, and where possessions were what mattered most. He had earned good money in Carácas, and he wasn't the kind to tuck his money away in a savings account. He had taken a flat in the neighbourhood called Las Colinas de Santa Monica, high on the green hills with a view out over the valley. He had come home every day with a new LP, because when the sun was throwing its last rays on the two-thousand-metre-high Avila, he liked to stand on the balcony and listen to the warm voice of Ella Fitzgerald, or to Chet Baker's long, raspy licks. He had driven around in a big limo and even had a plane at his disposal to fly to the Gran Sabana. As assistant manager at the Tamanaco he had money enough to spend, and could live with a certain jet-set élan – in the scrapbooks, I came across photos of Truffino leaning against a racecar.

During those years, Carácas had unmistakably taken on the allure of Los Angeles or Miami. With the mind-boggling oil revenues, the money came rolling in like in a casino. Nothing was too exorbitant, at least not for the moneyed, for Venezuela was South American enough to share the wealth as unequally as possible. The villas grew to the size of hunting lodges; the retail branch doing the best business was the marble trade. At the same time, Carácas was marked by a strikingly intellectual climate. In the 1930s, to escape the Spanish Civil War and Franco's regime, thousands of Spanish academics and left-wing activists had fled to Venezuela. In the 1940s, European exiles filled the ranks, and in the 1940s and 1950s came political refugees from other South American countries as well. As long as they didn't become involved in domestic politics, the military regime left them alone – to the outside world, Venezuela was pleased to hold up a façade of tolerance.

The Cuban writer Alejo Carpentier was one of the refugees who came to Venezuela. He arrived in Carácas in 1945, and taught for fourteen years at the Academy of Fine Arts. He took part in one of the first geographical expeditions to the Gran Sabana, and used his experiences in *Los pasos perdidos*, a novel about the jungle, about the relationship between whites and Indians, and about the primal forms of music; a novel which seems, in each and every line, to have served as an example to Truffino. There is the same astonishment at the Indians, the same respect, and the same belief in the power of the rugged nature of the Gran Sabana to summon up the strongest of aesthetic sensations. The book was published in 1953, but was more influential outside South America than on the continent itself. While Europe was scraping away the last of its debris and the threat of a new war loomed, a war that would undoubtedly be fought with nuclear weapons, Carpentier described a world as yet untouched, a world that was still largely undiscovered, that had not yet been made to conform to the Western way of thinking and living.

It was only in 1951 that a joint French-Venezuelan expedition to the depths of the Amazon Basin found the source of the Orinoco, one of South America's longest rivers. One more proof that, since Alexander von Humboldt and Aimé Bonpland's journey over the Orinoco and the Casiquiare, very little indeed had been added to what was known about the region. Von Humboldt and Bonpland had made that journey in the year 1800.

There was a rush on Venezuela by geographers, biologists and anthropologists. They came from every country in Europe and from the United States. Galfrid Dunsterville, the orchid expert, was among the first academic adventurers, as was biologist Otto Huber, and Julian Steyermark, a plant fanatic from Missouri whom the American government sent to the Gran Sabana in 1944 to find natural ingredients for quinine, which was in short supply because of the war in Asia. On the mesas he found so many endemic plants that he decided to dedicate the rest of his life to a study of Guyanese flora; he was the first person to do research into the plants which the Yonamami use for *yoppo*, a narcotic they administer by blowing it into each other's nostrils through a metre-long tube; he astonished his colleagues by estimating the number of plants found exclusively in the Gran Sabana at 9,400, then by adjusting that figure six months later to between twenty and thirty-five thousand, and starting on the systematic description of all the types, a project in which he involved one hundred and eighty botanists from all over the world. Steyermark, Dunsterville and Huber were all among Truffino's oldest friends in Venezuela.

As I leafed through his scrapbooks, I had the impression that Truffino had found it difficult to make a choice during his first years in Venezuela. He had no shortage of female companionship – a series of snapshots taken on the beaches behind the row of hills separating Carácas from the sea gave evidence of that. A somewhat larger photo shows Truffino himself, a cigarette in one corner of his mouth, his necktie loosened, shirtsleeves rolled up, left foot off the floor, a little bent over, wildly dancing the jive or the bebop... Another picture, from 1955, shows him playing the guitar while being stared at adoringly by a girl who looks rather like Audrey Hepburn. He must have enjoyed living in a city that combined North American progress with South American vivacity; it must have helped him forget the rigid country of his youth. And at the same time, it must have all been just a bit too tame; he barely had to prove himself in Carácas, he had succeeded even before he'd had a chance to be put to the test.

After his time with the Pemón, his doubts seem to have vanished. According to a clipping, a plane landed at Canaime (sic) on September 8th, 1956 and found there the Dutchman Rudolf J.M. Trufino (with only one f), who had been missing for eight months. After a bit of hesitation he had decided to fly back to Carácas, but by the end of that year he was back in Canaima with his guitar, a few tools, twelve crates of books and, this time, a radio transmitter, so he would never again be completely cut off from the world.

The next day Josef took me by boat to the Mayupa rapids. Legend has it that a woman once fell into the water there and survived, but emerged without (*pa*) her skirt (*mayu*). I was better able to understand the amazement at that miraculous survival as we approached the rapids; it had been raining all night, and the water roiled and whirled so fearfully that I was happy when Josef turned the *curiare* around and did not try to get any closer to the Mayupa.

He ran the dugout a little ways downriver, to a sandy beach. The sun broke through the clouds at last; I took off my clothes and dove into the water. Right away, fish began nibbling at my skin.

'There aren't piranhas here, are there?' I shouted to Josef.

He laughed loudly at that.

'They can't get past the falls at Canaima. They wouldn't fight their way up that.'

'But I'm being bitten by a whole school of fish.'

'They're sucking the salt off your body. They think you're a delicacy, Janito.'

He had started calling me Janito, I didn't understand exactly why, but whenever he said Janito he grinned from one floppy ear to the next.

A cloud slid in front of the sun, turning the water a darker shade: from tea-brown to coffee-brown.

'When some leaves and roots rot in the water,' Josef lectured me from the canoe, 'it creates a waste product, tannin, that makes the water acidic and gives it a dark colour. The acidity is extremely high, a pH of almost five. So there aren't many minerals, and not many plants either. The fish eat each other here, because there's no other food for them. Very little bacteria either, you can drink this water right out of the stream. And there's no salt at all, which is why the fish like to nibble at your arms and legs.'

Josef pulled the boat up onto the shore; I swam to the

beach, dried myself off and was immediately attacked by a cloud of sand fleas. Above my head a pair of ospreys were circling, further away the *zamuros* – black vultures – kept watch, and a sandy-coloured bird landed in the jasmine tree. Josef called it the 'nightwatcher'.

'There,' I said, pointing towards the savanna, 'was the airstrip where Baughan and Truffino landed.'

'How do you know that?' Josef asked, sounding slightly nettled. He took his task seriously, and he was the one who was supposed to do the explaining; it was already bad enough that I occasionally consulted *A Guide to the Birds of Venezuela*.

'I read it in Ruth Robertson's book. An American journalist who worked for the English-language newspaper in Carácas in the forties and fifties. She had Baughan drop her off once close to Mayupa.'

He didn't completely believe me.

'Have you seen Baughan's grave?' he asked.

'Where?'

'Close to the airstrip at Canaima.'

'That's impossible. Baughan crashed at Higuerote.'

'And what happened then?'

'No idea.'

Josef nodded contentedly. Now we had switched roles.

'After the time he stayed with the Indians, when he heard what had happened to Baughan, señor Rudy went into the mountains close to Higuerote and found the wreckage of Baughan's plane. He buried the bodies of the seven passengers – or what was left of them after ten months – on the spot; he had the remains of Charlie and Mary Baughan flown to Canaima, and buried them beside the airstrip, under a stone on which he had chiseled their names.'

Hearing that, I believe, was the first thing that made me want to write about Rudy Truffino.

Or maybe it was later, when I found Gerti's diary.

Or even later still, when I started realizing what an inhuman task it is to build something up in the jungle, and how miserably fast what you've achieved comes undone.

I was still the only guest at the camp. It couldn't be very profitable for Truffino to go up to Angels Falls only for me. Josef said five Americans were on their way, though; after they arrived, Truffino would be sure to join us. I figured he was in the capital on business, or visiting his daughter in Puerto Ordaz. Everything that was used and consumed at the camp had to be flown in from that town on the Orinoco, and Truffino usually did that himself, in his own Cessna.

I couldn't have arrived in the Gran Sabana at a worse moment. In May the rain falls from the sky by the bucketful.

'You should have come in March or April,' Josef would say whenever the sky clouded over. 'Or around New Year's.'

But back then I'd been working on the final chapters of a novel set at sea, and in my thoughts I had been travelling through another rugged and desolate place: the Straits of Magellan.

'From May up to the end of August it's really impossible. None of the rapids are navigable then. And this year is particularly rainy.'

It was May of 1995, a month in which all records were indeed broken.

The next morning I was awakened early by thousands of birds out on the savanna. There was no glass in the windows of my room, only screens. When I thought I heard a couple of parrots, I got up. It turned out to be macaws.

Once, in the Louvre, I had seen three macaws, painted by Pieter Boel, a 17th century Dutchman. Macaws with orangeish-red feathers. It was such a peculiarly warm tint that I had felt like taking the little oil painting (or was it a gouache? or a pastel?) down off the wall and giving it a place of the highest honour, on my wall at home. Now, some twenty years later, I saw it clearly again, and at the same time I remembered how back then I had immediately wanted to gather around me everything that spoke of the tropics. I missed a certain fervour in the Netherlands, in the landscape and the way of living, and unless I was sorely mistaken Truffino would know exactly what I meant when I told him about Boel's macaws.

The earliest morning sun cast an orange light on the savanna. To wake up quietly I went back to the gallery in front of my room and crawled into the hammock. Only minutes later did I become aware of an Indian girl, barely ten paces from where I lay, combing her hair. She had apparently just washed it in the river and let it dry while she sat on a flat stone in the early sunlight, and now she was combing it with long strokes; gleaming hair that reached down below her waist. With every stroke of the comb it grew darker, until finally it reached the deepest shade of black. Which reminded me of yet another painting, perhaps the dreamiest one Paul Gauguin ever painted on his South Sea island. He had called it '*Arearea*', 'Peace'.

Josef and I were planning to go to the Orchid Island, on the Rio Carrao, just a little north of the Auyán Tepui.

After breakfast, as we were about to leave, it started pouring.

'This is not going to be fun,' Josef sighed, buttoning up his plastic coat. When he climbed into the dugout, the water rose immediately to his ankles; I suggested we postpone the trip until the next day. 'You're an easy man to please, Janito. And at least you're not in a hurry.'

To express his thanks, he unlocked the library for me.

'You like books, right?' he asked as he turned the key and pushed open the door.

The first thing I saw was the skin of a jaguar, hanging on a clothesline stretched between the bookcases; the second was a collection of snakes in formaldehyde.

'This is a nice one,' Josef grinned. 'A *cascabel*, a rattlesnake. And this is the coral snake; step on this one and, as señor Rudy puts it, you've got four minutes to write your will. And here we have the dreaded bushmaster, a small one; bushmasters can grow up to three-and-a-half metres.'

It was a snake like this one that had bitten Truffino. According to Josef, he never talked about it much; just as he rarely recalled his accident with the rattlesnake, which had cost him part of his right earlobe. No, he continued to be amazed at the elegance with which these animals moved, and refused to participate in the phobia for snakes to which the Indians are also subject. The Pemón see in every case of snakebite the workings of the *canaima*.

'On one of the first trips I ever made with him, I almost stepped on a coral snake. I was getting ready to kill it right away, but señor Rudy stopped me. 'Look at it first,' he said. It was a non-venomous coral snake, which I should have seen by its rings; the non-poisonous variety usually has three rings in a row, a poisonous one usually has five. Señor Rudy took a whole series of pictures of it.'

The collection of gruesome insects contained scorpions and spiders in glass jars. The grand trophy was obviously the tarantula; the tapir skulls, lined up right behind it, looked friendly by comparison. This tarantula wasn't as big as the one Maria Sibylla Merian had drawn. Merian had gone into the jungles of Surinam to draw or make watercolours of everything she found creepy, fascinating or beautiful – a fairly unusual practice for a woman in 1705. The spider was also not as big as the one I'd heard Redmond O'Hanlon talk about, with a vague echo of panic in his voice, when I met him one time just after his journey through the Amazon jungle. 'It fell out of the tree my hammock was tied to. Fairly flat-shaped. The size of a dinner plate.'

Truffino's spider was no bigger than the palm of my hand, its legs about as long as my fingers. Each leg was covered in hundred of hairs, which must have made it quite a job to get it into the jar; every hair on the tarantula is poisonous. Their bite is not much more dangerous than a hornet sting, though, and they only bite when they feel threatened. At night tarantulas pounce on their prey, usually small birds brooding in their nests.

I asked Josef whether living here wasn't a constant nightmare.

'What do you mean?' he asked, sincerely baffled.

'You can't tell me that you enjoy encountering a hairy monster like this? Or whatever it was that used to wear this lovely skin… What is it, anyway?'

'An anaconda.'

Yes, of course. What would the South American jungle be without the anaconda? It was definitely at home in this shop of horrors.

'But then,' I posited, 'I suppose you have to go awfully deep into the jungle to find one.'

'Oh no. Gerti shot this one right in front of the door. Rudy was on the Auyán Tepui, and she was alone here with the children. When an anaconda's hungry, it will swallow a little girl just like that. Especially one this size.'

'How big was it?'

'Eight and a half metres.'

'Holy shit. And I could trip over one of those tonight?'

'This one was down by the stream that runs close to your room. Anacondas are water snakes.'

'Is there anything here that *isn't* dangerous?'

'The orchids, Janito. It's May now, so if we're lucky they'll be blooming on Orchid Island. And the butterflies. Like these.'

He pointed to five glass cases containing about a hundred and fifty specimens, pinned neatly to a bed of silk.

'This one, for example' – the colours were dazzling – 'isn't in any butterfly guide. This one isn't either. Or this one. Señor Rudy caught all three of them on top of the Auyán Tepui. Most of the other ones were caught by Lily, his oldest daughter. A real jungle girl; she's crazy about butterflies, but she'll pick up a coral snake and let it crawl up her arm.'

I shuddered.

'The butterfly cases,' Josef went on imperturbably, 'should actually go to some museum of natural history.'

The same applied to the stone axes, which were prehistoric Pemón relics, and the first spears to which they had ever attached iron heads – they should all go straight to an ethnological museum.

Josef swept aside a spider web and led me to the library itself, ten bookcases set up in rows like in a real library. Between the rows stood a huge table on which the Märklin trains had once torn past stations, through switchyards and under mountains, crepe-paper mountains.

'Those three girls of Rudy's had to play too sometimes, and he raised them like boys. They've turned out tough. I hope you never run into one of them, or at least, that if you do you don't get in a fight with them.'

He was piquing my curiosity.

Amid the model trains lay a toy pistol, close to the little station was a real pistol. I picked it up and held it to my temple.

'Hey, be careful,' Josef said. 'This is South America, you know; it could be loaded.'

I handed it to him, and he clicked open the cylinder.

'Bravo, Janito.'

It was loaded.

'I think you're better off keeping your nose in the books.'

There were thousands of them, and they hadn't been dusted in years. During the dry season the dust must have blown in there in clouds. There was no glass in the windows of the library either; behind the screens, however, finger-thick steel cable had been stretched to keep out the mice and rats.

I picked up the first volume of *Del Roraima al Orinoco*, Theodor Koch-Grünberg's standard work on the Indians of southwestern Venezuela. Through it, the termites had left a trail of abuse; the other two volumes were in little better shape, half-devoured, turned to powder.

'You'll have a wonderful time in here,' Josef predicted.

As soon as he was gone I walked straight to a bookcase all the way at the back, which contained piles of newspapers, piles of letters and piles of bills. It was unmistakably the bookcase containing the personalia. Under a couple of orange-covered boxes, originally intended for photographic paper, I discovered a fat black book with a burlap-coloured linen cover. I opened it and saw a picture of a jaguar swimming across a river. Closer to the front, the pictures were of snowy mountaintops and young men on skis, little pictures circled in pencil, three or four to a page. Between those photos was the text in royal blue ink, written in an orderly, cursive hand, in German.

It was Gerti's diary.

Gertraud Koppenwallner's father was a goldsmith, and had his shop in the old centre of Salzburg, on Klampfergasse. He had inherited the business from his father. It must have been a rather presitigious firm: in 1984, when the business celebrated its hundredth anniversary, the family offered the people of Salzburg a free concert by Concentus Musicus, directed by Nikolaus Harnoncourt. The program consisted entirely – what else would one expect in Salzburg? – of Mozart. Gerti had put the program in the little box I found beneath her diary, plus the printed concert invitation showing the outside of her father's store. For a jeweller's, the storefront looked strikingly austere.

There wasn't much about her earliest years. The first part of the diary wasn't in the bookcase, and I never found it later amid the piles of papers. The second part begins in 1954; Gerti is twenty-three, and working as a licensed goldsmith in her father's shop.

A happy Austrian youth – at least, that's the impression given in the sturdy pages of her diary, which had survived even the tropics. Not a single untoward comment, and when a complaint is made, it lacks all sting. Skiing on the Schmittenhöhe, taking part in races at Bad Gastein or Kitzbühel, slaloming. The weather is always nice, *Licht und Luft und Sonne*, the snow ranges from *schön* to *wunderschön*, the ski runs are *bald recht gut ausgefahren*, and the young men whose pictures she takes are all in ruddy good health. The age of the fashionable ski-suit has not yet arrived, the men wear corduroy trousers, zip-up turtlenecks and suede gloves, and they look like Gregory Peck in *Spellbound*. She lets herself be immortalized on the slopes of St. Cristoph am Arlberg, her back straight and proud, her long legs bent slightly at the knees, her dark-blond hair pulled back tight, and then she does slightly resemble Gregory Peck's co-star, Ingrid Bergman.

Maiskogel, Mitterfeldarm, Loferer Alm, Jenner, Watzmannhar, Tavern – she was out skiing almost every weekend. In the summer she took long hikes in Adnet-Nesselgraben, along the Königsee or the Mattsee. Occasionally a boyfriend shows up more frequently in the photos, lays his head somewhat coyly in her lap, then vanishes from sight again, despite the *schöne Aussichten*. The pangs of love are barely mentioned, for fear that *dieses Buch in unrechte Hände käme*.

In 1954 she spends the summer in Italy, in 1955 she and her friend Ilse drive the newest-model Opel to Yugoslavia. In another picture she is standing beside her scooter, a Vespa; her father apparently paid her well for the jewellery she made. In love, however, things do not go so very well, which prompts her to switch at times to French. '*Chacun a son goût,*' she notes after a Sunday on the Fuschlsee that didn't turn out the way she'd hoped.

The tone of her writing suddenly becomes much keener when she receives a letter from Venezuela, offering her a position with Leiser Import in Carácas. The diary doesn't make clear how she came in contact with the firm, or exactly what she hoped to do there. Mention is made of an Aunt

Lolita who is married to a Venezuelan; Uncle Otto appears in the photos of a party for the Leiser employees. Perhaps he was the link between Salzburg and Carácas.

From one of the first magazine articles about the Truffinos, I gathered that Gerti had been taken on primarily to assay the quality of the gems that were to be shipped to Europe. There was a great deal of rubbish among it, and there was no need to go to the trouble of having that cleared by customs, with its muddle of forms, documents and official stamps. She was an expert: at a single glance, she could separate the wheat from the chaff. But soon she was to become a *Mädchen für alles*, and spent most of her time typing letters.

Before leaving for Venezuela, she climbs 'her' mountain – the Predigtstuhl – one last time. To lend added lustre to her farewell, she dresses up in a Tyrolean skirt and blouse. The next photos show her wearing tight pants that reach halfway down her calves, and she will continue to wear pants of that type until she goes into the jungle. There, she prefers overalls.

Atop the Predigtstuhl the sun is shining, the mist remains hanging in the valley. She is annoyed by the 'Sunday mountain climbers'; it is still early afternoon when she suggests to her friends that they begin the descent. Without being overly dramatic, she realizes full well how final this farewell is: '*Mit unseren Bergtouren wird es nun für immer aus sein!*'

The same friends see her off in Genoa. Max – who appears in many of the photos – has a hard time believing she's really leaving; only when he sees her bulging suitcases does it sink in that she is truly emigrating. As they drive out of Salzburg, the sky above the city is bluer than ever. A hundred kilometres down the road, that has all been relegated to the domain of memory; she revels in South Tyrol, the Brenner Pass, Lake Garda. For someone moving to the other side of the world, she behaves with remarkable coolness. Or has she grown tired of Europe?

When the war broke out she was nine years old; by the end of the war, almost fifteen. During the first post-war years, even at the foot of the white mountains, Austria must have been a drab place. Nowhere in her diaries does she refer to that period; she keeps her eyes fixed on the present, or on the future. When the news comes from Venezuela, she seems to be in a hurry to leave the Old World behind.

In Genoa she has to wait three days for her ship to sail. Her friends return to Salzburg, and then she is briefly overcome by the feeling that everything around her has become empty. 'A funny feeling,' she adds promptly.

Like all emigrants leaving Europe from Genoa, she visits the churchyard, where the graves lend death a baroque splendor. As a woman alone, she can't go out at night into the harbour town; she hangs around a bit in the hotel lounge, until she meets an Arab, 'or, in any case, a Mohammedan'. He takes her out with him, and even when they dance he behaves with 'French gallantry'.

She sails aboard the Franca C. by way of Barcelona and Tenerife to La Guaira. Although she travels first class, she shares a cabin with three other passengers. Whenever one of the women wants to wash herself or get dressed, the others must go onto the deck; then she understands why Italian passenger liners are referred to as 'spaghetti cruisers'.

Passing through the Straits of Gibraltar, she wonders when she will see Europe again. It is her only moment of doubt.

After Tenerife she spends an evening talking to a young Greek who has studied physics, and who hopes to find a job in the oil business. Along with his aunt he is on his way to Maracaibo. On the day the ship is to enter the harbour at La

Guaira, he has a note delivered to her cabin at 7.55 a.m. 'Bye-bye and a very good luck. I wish you. Andy.'

In Carácas, she spends a few months at her Aunt Lolita's house. The bougainvillea blooms around the bungalow the whole year round, parked before the door is a white Studebaker.

Gerti earns three hundred bolivars a month; by the end of the year that has been raised to seven hundred. After eight days in Carácas she already feels like a part of the city, although she doesn't yet speak a word of Spanish. The process of emigration all goes with amazing ease. She swims in the pool at the Tamanaco Hotel, which looks out over the entire city, allows Aunt Lolita to drag her from one cocktail party to the next, wears a revealing dress to the *Gran Baile de Gala*, which is officially opened by the president of the republic. She describes it as in a dream, the Mexican orchestra, the orchids on the walls, the tuxedos and the gala uniforms, the diamonds too big for one finger, and the autograph hounds surrounding the Hollywood stars Terry Moore, Rita Moreno, Donna Reed and Russ Tennblyer, whose glamour brightens up the ball.

In late 1956 Leiser Import sends her to Maracaibo; on February 10th she flies to Canaima. Reason: unknown. She is the sole passenger on the flight from Puerto Ordaz to Canaima; from the air she sees a few Indian settlements, and a few forest fires.

At Canaima she finds two Dutchmen, three children, a Negress from Trinidad, two dogs and a parrot named Elvis. She sleeps in the Captain's Quarters, the hut that once belonged to Charlie Baughan.

On her trip to an Indian village she is accompanied by '*Rudi, der Holländer*'. The first thing that impresses her about him is that he speaks the language of the Indians as though he'd been raised among them; the second, that he does not hesitate long before pulling a trigger. Rudy shoots a *gallito de las rocas* and roasts it over the fire; after the meal is over he picks up his guitar. As soon as darkness falls, he gets ready to leave for Ucaima, where he has a hut he uses for hunting – she asks to go with him.

In an old jeep with broken headlights they drive southward through the tall grass of the savanna. To follow the tracks through the grass, she remains standing upright in the jeep, holding a flashlight into each hand. Sometimes they stop to relish the silence or, as she puts it, '*von der Natur in ihrer tiefsten Seele*'. Rudy shoots a fox, then drives on to a cave where they can hear the scorpions chirping. They climb out, walk to a round hut left behind by the Indians. On the pitch black path, Rudy suddenly stops; above the peeping of the bats he can hear another sound; a little later, she thinks she hears water moving; they must be close to a stream or a pool. For a while it remains quiet, then they hear a faint rustling. The third time they hear it, it's closer, behind them now. If it really is a jaguar, as Rudy thinks, then they had better call on their guardian angel: Rudy is carrying only a low calibre rifle, she has only a pocketknife. Jaguars apparently do not attack when they hear the cry of the *tantas*, and Rudy imitates it. To even his own amazement, a long silence follows.

He shines his flashlight along the trees. They see nothing. As they walk back to the jeep they hear a slight rustling again. Rudy starts the engine; at the same moment, behind them, along the river, they hear a jaguar wail. Jaguars wail when they're hungry. A little further along they hear another one. They wait in the car for half an hour. Then they hear a third jaguar wail. 'It sounds like the crying of a baby,' she writes.

Gerti stays at Canaima for fourteen days. She helps Rudy

build a hut, learns to drive a jeep across the savanna, and goes back to the Indian village, where she photographs the villagers' daily activities. It was to be the oldest film material of the Pemón who live around Canaima; disarming photos of men and women who have never before looked into the lens of a camera, and who do so with great timidity.

On her last night it is so hot that she decides to sleep outside in a hammock. The moon is unbelievably bright. In the middle of the night she awakes; her shirt is wet, her hand is sticky. When she turns on the flashlight, she sees that her wrist and arm are covered in blood. She uses her shirt to wipe away the blood, but doesn't see a cut. Her scream wakes Rudy, she jumps out of the hammock, runs into the hut and sees, in the mirror there, a tiny hole in one of her arteries. Blood is flowing from it.

Rudy ties up the bleeding artery, cleans the wound with alcohol. She supposes that he, as 'a certified veterinarian', must know what he's doing. At first he doesn't tell her what has happened, he waits half an hour and then, after he has stopped the bleeding, he says it with a grin, so as not to frighten her too badly: in her sleep, she has been bitten by a vampire bat. Of the hundred different types of bats common to South America, six or seven feed on blood. A little later, as she washes herself, she sees another little hole in her toe; a bat has bitten her there as well, but she had apparently pulled her foot away before the vampire could draw blood.

None of this makes her afraid of the jungle. It seems that, when it comes to animals, there is nothing that frightens her. Back in Carácas she moves into an apartment of her own, where she lets the cayman she brought back with her from the jungle – the amphibian measures almost two metres in length – walk around freely. The cayman likes to nibble amiably on her finger. For a treat, she goes to a pet shop and buys it a big, fat mouse. Two months later the mouse is still scurrying around the apartment. On the walls she hangs a great many '*Indianersachen*', which gives the apartment a 'belligerent feel'. And that pleases her.

On August 29th she is back at Canaima. There she will remain until October 7th, 1957. From Carácas she flies to the Gran Sabana with two men; one of them is Venezuelan, the other is the Dutchman 'everyone calls "Jungle Rudy"'. She has two film cameras with her, a professional 16 mm Bollex Paillard and an 8 mm one, and two still cameras as well, one for black and white and the other for colour. In her diary she writes down the various camera angles; with Rudy, she has hatched a plan to make a movie about Canaima.

Her urge to document becomes clearer all the time. Her diary ends with the story of the January 1958 revolution, which was started by students to put an end to the dictatorship of Pérez Jiménez – at the end of that same month, the general fled to the Dominican Republic. She follows the events like a real reporter. Although a curfew is in force, she drives around the city day and night to photograph the overturned cars, the burning buses, the tanks on street corners, the wounded looters, the graffiti on the walls, the ecstatic students, the pamphlets from La Junta Patriotica, the plundered shops, the jailbreak by political prisoners who, barely out of their cells, turn and burn down the prison, the attack on the headquarters of the Security Police, the attack on the brothel across the street from the *Seguridad*, with the intruders breaking the furniture to bits and molesting the whores...

With the same enthusiasm she describes her trip with Rudy to Angel Falls. It's raining hard, it takes them four days to drag the *curiare* through the rapids. The water rises fast, they find a sandy beach and put up their tents, but while they are preparing dinner they find themselves in water up to their waists. Just before dark they set up another camp in the pouring rain, kilometres further upriver; that night they sleep in wet clothes. When they finally reach Angel Falls, they perform an Indian dance in the canoe.

At the falls they climb part of the way up the wall of the mesa; Rudy must have already cut the path with his machete. The next day they head back downriver. They have to be quick about it, though, the water is rising all the time, and in the rapids the boat is tossed back and forth helplessly between the sharp rocks. But then the clouds part suddenly and turn white and they see a tapir swimming across the river. Behind them the water is crashing down amid shafts of sunlight. 'A sight so beautiful is a gift not given to many.' Finally they reach Rudy's hut at Ucaima, where they join in with the Indians in an all-night *cachiri* party. 'An extremely wild occasion.'

On February 23rd, 1958 she is back in Canaima once more. There she remains until March 9th. If she has not yet given her heart to Rudy by that point, then certainly to the Gran Sabana. Nowhere are the orchids more plentiful, and she has developed a true passion for orchids. Nowhere is nature more ominous, and the more savage the surroundings, the more she is in her element.

Six pages of her diary are covered with photos of the trip she made with Rudy to the Auyán Tepui. The last photo shows the head of a jaguar that is swimming across the river. But the text is missing.

From then on, I suspected, she'd had no more time for making notes, for she was too busy getting closer to Rudy. Later, though, I found the text that went with the photos, a text that was typed out, probably for a magazine – at that time, she clearly had journalistic ambitions.

After those pages containing only photos comes the description of the January revolution.

The final entry in the diary is a pressed orchid.

One year later, in the San José Cathedral in Carácas, she marries *'el caballero holandés señor Rudolf J. Truffino van der Luijt'*, as the *Ultima Noticias* of January 21st, 1959 reports. The service is held in German.

The gossip column of *The Daily News*, Carácas' English language daily, also mentions the wedding. 'Gerti,' the columnist wonders aloud, clearly aware of Truffino's reputation, 'does she wear black garters?'

In the photo I found among the clippings, she is wearing a wide dress. Six months later, the first child is born.

That night the river flooded its banks. I was afraid we were trapped at the camp now, but the next morning the sun was shining and we were finally able to take the boat to Orchid Island.

The dogs barked wildly as we loaded our supplies into the *curiare*. For the largest of the two, Tièta, a cross between a Saint Bernard and a Great Dane, I always stepped back in deference: he didn't even have to stand on his hind legs to poke his head into my ribcage. He had big black scabs on his legs.

'Vampire bites,' Josef told me.

As the experienced bowman, he took his place at the front of the *curiare*. At the outboard motor was a little, thickset Indian, whose name was José Castro.

'Any family of Lola?'

He looked at me as though I was prying in his family secrets.

The Mayupa was unassailable, a few kilometres before the rapids we had to pull the boat onto the shore. José took the outboard off its mounts and lifted it to his shoulder, Josef took the two cans of gasoline, I carried the cooler with supplies. We walked across the savanna for almost an hour, until we were past the second set of rapids, at a bend in the river. There, another boat was waiting for us.

The grass of the savanna was strange grass indeed. Around the tussocks all the soil had been washed away, the roots stuck out a few centimetres above the surface and, after forming a bulge, turned into hairy grass. There were always a few centimetres between the tussocks, which made it feel like walking over a field of mushrooms. The grass seemed unable to decide whether to be green or yellow. Every two or three metres was a plant with rugged leaves, thin red shoots and flowers that were emphatically yellow. Further along, yellowish fingers emerged from the grass.

'Bromeliads,' Josef panted, putting down the gas cans for a moment. '*Brocchinia reducta.* This is the only place it grows.'

The grasshoppers were troublesome; dozens of them came flying up at every step. The wind coming up over the savanna gave the insects a flying start; they bounced off our legs, our stomachs, our chests, and whenever they hit you in the hand or face it was like being whipped with a rope.

'Don't take off your sunglasses,' Josef called to me. 'Otherwise you'll get one in the eye and tomorrow everyone will be asking me whether you had a fight with your girlfriend.'

Castro was well prepared for the plague; before we started walking, he had tied a handkerchief over his nose and mouth. When we arrived at the river, he took off the handkerchief and could finally say what had been on his mind the whole time.

'My grandmother.'

Lola Castro was his grandmother.

His father had worked for Truffino, his brother had worked for Truffino, and one of his cousins had worked for Truffino too. Ever since Lola Castro had given the white man something to eat, there had been a Castro accompanying Truffino as his boatsman.

'That's wonderful.'

'Well, it depends who it was for. Tight, if you know what I mean.'

. I didn't, not until Josef translated it for me into English.

'His wife,' Josef added. 'They say señora Gerti squeezed every bolivar till it bled.'

'When did she die, anyway?'

'About ten years ago.'

'At Ucaima?'

'No, she went back to her own country. She was from Germany, right?'

That's how it goes when you leave home: after a while, no one really knows where you came from.

José attached the outboard to the second boat, and for the next few hours the *curiare* bucked its way upstream.

The jungle stretched out on both sides of the broad river. It looked friendlier than the tropical rainforest I'd travelled through in equatorial Africa; the trees here didn't reach for the clouds, the tallest among them was barely ten metres high, and close to the banks I estimated them at six or seven. In addition, most of them were parasol-shaped, and there were no nets of vines hanging in their branches. The ominous thing, however, was the background; after every bend in the river the walls of the Auyán Tepui rose up, walls the jungle tried to climb without ever reaching the top.

I barely looked at the water and the birds swooping past as we headed upriver, I couldn't take my eyes off that fabulous mountain. When Alejo Carpentier saw his first mesa looming up, his memory could only find something that looked like what he was seeing with his own eyes by taking him back to Jeroen Bosch, to the imaginary Babels portrayed by the painters of the fantastic, to the hallucinating illustrators of the temptations of the saints. And just when he thought he'd found an analogy (he also compared the *tepuis* to a city of Titans, with cylopic stairways, mausoleums for gigantic

72

creatures, ramparts of obsidian), he had to reject it again right away, because the proportions fell short of reality. It seemed to him that the mountains guarded the access to some kingdom forbidden to men; Von Humboldt, too, as he approached the southernmost mesa over the Casiquiare, sought in vain for any signs of human power.

The colour of the rock walls was in constant flux: one moment they were red, the next brown, and when a cloud formation tempered the light they could suddenly turn a grim black. The longer we moved past the mesa, the more deeply it impressed me with its unrelenting grandeur. The rains of hundreds of thousands of years had washed the sides clean, until only the most elemental remained: rock. With its bare vertical walls, the Auyán Tepui did indeed summon up associations with a building, and that building towered so high above the forest that its architect could only have his seat in the heavens.

We pulled the boat onto a narrow sandy beach beside an Indian camp. José asked the Pemón to build a fire on which we could roast our chicken; in return, he offered them three chickens and twelve cans of beer. This caused the men and women to hop out of their hammocks immediately, especially the offer of beer, which they quaffed back with all due speed.

I walked a little way into the forest, looking for the remains of the little Spanish chapel Gerti had found here during her first trip with Rudy. It must have been built by the Capuchin monks. In 1772, one of them, Brother Carlos de Barcelona, was the first to write the name Auyán on a map. The area around it, however, he marked as *Tierras Desiertas*. In the 19th century, the monks were forced to withdraw from the Gran Sabana and almost all the Venezuelan provinces: first their lives were endangered by Simón Bolivar's war of liberation, which was followed by seven hundred and thirty armed conflicts, twenty-six uprisings and a civil war that lasted five years and took forty-thousand lives. In addition, by the late 19th century a strong anti-clerical movement was underway in Venezuela, with political support at the highest levels; the president himself gave orders to raze as many cloisters and abbeys as possible. It was only under his successor that the Capuchins were able to continue their work – which was, in fact, every bit as destructive – and halfway through the 20th century they finally succeeded in converting the last of the Pemón to Christianity, by letting them perform chores in exchange for fishhooks. From that point on, the Indians introduced a new word into their own language, the Spanish *trabajar*; before that, they had referred to work only as 'doing something'.

Even fourteen years ago, not much was left of the little chapel as Gerti described it; since then the jungle must have muffled away the rest beneath a carpet of ferns and bushes. I, at least, could find no trace of it.

Back at the camp on the river, two children looked at me from their hammock as guilelessly as they must have looked at Truffino in 1956. Only when I pulled out my camera did their eyes betray a slight panic, which reminded me of Gerti's photos. Rudy and Gerti had undeniably become my invisible travelling companions, and I journeyed with them, through time.

The chicken tasted of the coconut husks over which it had been roasted. Scratching about in the jungle had obviously given the bird a pair of juicy and sinewy legs. I wasn't the only one who felt like gnawing the drumstick to the bone: from a bush, a toucan came hopping over to me, purplish-blue spots around its eyes, a white breast, an orangeish-red backside and a yellow spot just under the tail. Its beak, almost as big as its body, snapped at my ankle; I jumped, the toucan flew up and

tore the piece of chicken out of my hand. 'Bravo!' Josef and
José shouted, applauding loudly, and I began to understand
why Truffino had felt so much at home among the Pemón;
they are a people who obtain maximum pleasure from the
slightest diversion.

After dinner, we crossed the river. Josef had not been
exaggerating, there were at least ten orchids growing on every
tree, some of them as tiny as the head of a pin, others with huge
purple blossoms. One out of every five orchids was in bloom.

Just before Orchid Island the Rio Carrao splits, then
regroups on the other side. The left arm of the river is very
narrow; when we arrived at the south end of the island, we
were able to wade across. The water came up no further than
our knees, and only in the middle were we forced to hop from
stone to stone.

Up against the bottom of the Auyán Tepui I picked out a
pair of huts with walls of bamboo slats and sheets of
corrugated iron nailed together crookedly. Long tree roots
held the pointed roofs in place; they were lashed across the
corrugated iron sheets like ropes.

'That's where Alejandro Laime lived,' Josef said.

'Lived?'

'He died last month.'

I had come across his name repeatedly in magazine articles,
and in Ruth Robertson's book *Churún Merú – The Tallest Angel*.

Aleksander Laime was born in Lithuania. At the start of
World War Two, out of antipathy towards the Russians who
had annexed his country, he chose to fight along with the
Nazis. He volunteered for the SS, and came to regret that
halfway through the war. In 1942 or 1943, he deserted, and
popped up in Venezuela in 1945.

According to some sources, he was a cartographer by

profession and had taken part in an expedition organized by the Venezuelan government for the purpose of charting the Gran Sabana. Ruth Robertson supplied a different version: according to her, Laime had graduated from the University of Riga with a degree in mining engineering.

Robertson chose Laime as her guide on her expedition to establish the precise height of Angels Falls. In 1949 she had Charlie Baughan drop her off close to the Mayupa rapids. By that time Laime had been living for several years on the banks of the Rio Carrao, across from Orchid Island, though he was also sighted, albeit sporadically, in Carácas in the late 1940s. Robertson's description is that of a man at odds with himself, but one who wished to bother other people with that as little as possible. She had to prise every word from his mouth, and that drove the loquacious American to despair.

By the time Truffino arrived at Canaima, Laime had severed all bonds with the world. He lived alone and maintained infrequent contact even with the Indians. Once every few months he would canoe down to Canaima to sell the gems he had found in the rivers and streams around his two huts. He used the money to buy salt, sugar, bullets, fishing line, gasoline and other things needed to survive in an area without another mortal soul for sixty kilometres around.

The photos in Robertson's book show a sturdy man in his forties, with square shoulders, a broad chest, a considerable tummy, a thick tassel of hair and a neatly trimmed fringe of beard. Later, when he began feeding himself exclusively on plants and mushrooms and fasting for days on end, he became as gaunt and lean as Truffino.

From Josef I heard that another hermit had once lived close to Canaima; Anyatoli, a Russian. No one knew why he had come to Venezuela, The only thing he ever said about it was that he hated Bolsheviks. He avoided people entirely, and spent his days drinking. Once, when an anaconda had seized Anyatoli from behind, Truffino had saved his life; he shot the snake through the head. After that they decided to set up a field telephone, so they could warn each other in an emergency. Once the ten-kilometre-long cable had been laid through the jungle, Anyatoli would occasionally crank up the phone to inform Truffino that he had caught a big fish; they would then eat the fish together, but in silence. Soon, the telephone stopped ringing altogether: the Indians had cut the cable into pieces for fishing line.

The contact between Truffino and Anyatoli was never very close; it is, after all, fairly impossible to carry on a real conversation with a taciturn drunkard. But between Laime and Truffino there soon arose something like mutual respect; that they were able to communicate effortlessly in German may have helped as well.

Laime, Josef told me, had explored the *tepuis* on his own, climbed the highest rocks, brought back plants no one had ever seen before, dissected them, developed theories. Atop the Auyán Tepui he had come across certain creatures that were a mystery to him. Truffino was the only one he could talk to about it, for in the chasms and crevasses Truffino, too, had seen remarkable shapes go shooting off, things that made him wonder whether he was dreaming with his eyes open, or whether he had somehow penetrated deep into the primordial. They traded observations, to get a more complete picture of what they had seen only at a glance.

The two men met up only once every two or three months, never more often than that.

'They understood each other very well,' Josef said, 'but they couldn't stand each other. At first, Laime knew a lot more about the area. But it wasn't long before Truffino caught up with him. Truffino was in constant contact with the scientists who came to the Gran Sabana; he heard a lot of things from Dunsterville, Steyermark and Huber, who also sent him their latest scientific publications. Laime gradually fell behind. But he considered himself much more authentic than Truffino, purer. Through Truffino, more and more foreigners started coming to the area, scientists at first, but later tourists too, and Laime hated the common herd.'

What irritated him most was that Truffino, more than just a guide or a source of information, had become what he had actually hoped to be – the oracle of the Gran Sabana.

'After 1962, the relationship became a lot more strained. The area around Canaima, including the Auyán Tepui, was declared a national park, and the government appointed Rudy Truffino as park director. It was the crowning glory for Truffino's pioneering work, but Laime felt that the crown really belonged to him.'

Walking beneath big mango trees, we entered the grounds. In the first hut we came to, everything had been rifled. Not only had the books been pulled off the shelf and opened, they had even been torn from their covers and ripped apart. The cupboard with supplies had been pushed over, the packs of flour and sugar torn open, the pots and pans flattened. Boxes had been upended, clothing torn to shreds.

The second hut wasn't much better. Everything that had been in racks was on the ground, and that ground, which had been covered only by a few reed mats, had been dug up and had deep holes in it.

'Why did they do this?' I asked Josef.

'Jewels. Gold nuggets. Right after he died, the looters came in. They were hoping to find a fortune.'

'Indians?'

He nodded.

The Pemón may not have valued property, but this bore witness to disgusting greed.

A piece of cardboard was nailed to one of the poles, and on it, in big letters, a poem was written:

Up the airy mountain
Down the rushy glen
We daren't go a hunting
For fear of little men…

… Imavary

I asked Josef how old Laime was when he died.

'About eighty-five.'

Of those eight-five years, he had spent fifty in these huts.

I squatted down, picked up a book, opened it. It was the fourth volume of Von Humbold's thirteen-part travelogue about his journey though South and Central America. In the margins of this German-language edition were dozens of notes, some of them in Spanish, written in scratchy pencil strokes. The sentences that had been underlined all spoke of the feeling that overcame Von Humboldt regularly as he travelled over the Río Negro and the Casiquiare: that man meant nothing compared to the jungle that surrounded him.

It didn't really surprise me that Laime, in his total isolation, had looked for solace from a scholar who had played a pioneering role in geology, botany, zoology, anthropology, archaeology, oceanography and meteorology. Back in Europe, Von Humboldt enjoyed the upright admiration of both Goethe and Chateaubriand, and Napoleon had granted him a private audience. (Napoleon to Von Humboldt: 'So you're interested in plants? So is my wife!') But Laime gradually came to resemble more closely Von Humboldt's travelling companion, Aimée Bonpland. The Frenchman returned to South America in the hope of finding a teaching position, was imprisoned for nine years by the paranoid dictator of Paraguay, and ended his life, at the age of eighty-five, close to the Uruguayan-Brazilian border, in a muddy hut amid plants and children he had begotten by his Indian housekeeper.

Around Laime's hut there were not even flowers or children.

'He couldn't stand having anyone around,' Josef told me. 'I went to see him three or four times. He took the salt I'd brought for him, nodded, then walked back to the river, where he sat down on a stone in a little set of rapids, looking for something shiny, without saying a word.'

At the end of the afternoon, as we boated our way back, I felt an intense loneliness rise up in me under a glowing sky.

As soon as Truffino finished building the camp at Canaima, Avensa became interested in it. The airline management's attention was drawn to the region by the American filmmaker Lowell Thomas and biologist Thomas E. Gilliard of New York's Museum of Natural History, who had travelled to southeastern Venezuela to make a documentary about the Auyán Tepui. The production was financed by the CBS broadcasting company and *Life* magazine. A crew of the size fitting for a Hollywood production came to Canaima. Avensa provided the transportation; Truffino put up the film crew and assumed daily leadership of the expedition, for which three months had been reserved. Speculating on the promotional effect of the documentary and the article in *Life*, Avensa began flying once a week from Carácas to Canaima, with a DC3. The trip took a little over four hours.

Aboard one of the first flights to the Gran Sabana were Jean-Louis Barrault and his wife, the actress Madeleine Renaud. Just before the war, Barrault had become famous with his role in the cult classic *Les enfants du paradis*. After travelling with Truffino to Orchid Island, he tore a page from his pocket diary and wrote on it: *Souvenir de deux jours au vrai Paradis*.

The next guest who could barely find words to express his enthrallment was the scientist and mountain climber Nicholas J. Piantanida, of New Jersey. In late 1956, he and Truffino had climbed the north face of the Auyán Tepui. In January of 1959, the two of them went looking for a waterfall which the Indians claimed was even higher than the Salto Angel. They never found it; they did, however, penetrate more deeply into Churún Canyon than anyone had before.

During the Christmas season of 1958, Truffino went on his first expedition with Stalky and Nora Dunsterville; precisely one year later he returned with the Dunstervilles to the Auyán Tepui, for the purpose of collecting as many new types of orchids as possible. They were difficult journeys, as attested to by a letter Mrs. Dunsterville sent Truffino a few months later. 'What we keep looking for,' she wrote, 'is that one, unexpected moment of happiness that we find in the wilderness. That moment was the generous reward for weeks of misery.'

In that same year Truffino welcomed Professor J. van Oord of Leiden University. The exact purpose of the famous astronomer's visit to the Guyanese highlands was something I could not figure out; nowhere else, however, could he have found a better place to get close to the heavens. One clear evening I stood on the riverbank and saw, for the first time with my own eyes, the reason why our galaxy is called the 'Milky Way'. Nowhere, not even in the desert, not even in the middle of the ocean, have I ever seen as clearly as I did above the Río Carrao the white streak set off against the firmament – like a trail of milk, indeed.

'That which one usually sees in the movie theatres,' Professor Van Oord wrote in the guestbook, 'is what Rudy F.M. Truffino has shown to us. But the difference is that, this time, it was reality, not just an image of it. And it is precisely the search for reality, as Rudy, living with his young family in the jungle has realized so well, that gives life its value.'

In March of 1960 the Venezuelan scientist and explorer Félix Cardona Puig spent a few weeks at the camp. As early as 1936, Cardona had found a way to climb the south face of the Auyán Tepui, but now he had come to see the progress Truffino had made on the north face.

During that same year, another American film crew arrived at Canaima, this time to shoot a feature film based on the novel *Green Mansions* by W.H. Hudson. The leading role was played by Audrey Hepburn. Rudy was allowed to stand in her shadow: he had a bit part, as a hunter.

Facilities at the camp were primitive; the hut where Truffino slept had no walls, from the roof to the ground was only a layer of mosquito netting. The guesthouses were rudimentary as well, wooden cottages with roofs of palm fronds. In *Tristes tropiques*, Claude Lévi-Strauss wrote that living in the jungle always reminded him of being in the army. Looking at the first photos taken of Canaima, I arrived at the same conclusion: those who visited there had no choice but to submit to the regime of a recruit on bivouac. Nevertheless, the first visitors waxed lyrical about the atmosphere at the camp, and that could only have been due to Truffino's charisma. To the Americans he became 'Jungle Rudy', and the woman who ran things in his absence was soon 'Savannah Gerti.' The names spoke of affection, and of respect.

Success never meets with gratitude, but when it overcomes a foreigner he can count on envy. The growing number of visitors proved that there was money to be made at Canaima. The breathtakingly beautiful spot on the lagoon also offered the opportunity for a much more sizeable project. Henry Boulton, one of the richest men in Venezuela and owner of Avensa, among other holdings, became interested in it. He decided to build a hotel complex with ninety bungalows right across from the waterfall, on the very spot where Truffino had his camp.

After Baughan's death, there were four participants in the limited company that owned Canaima: the German Hans Heimadinger and his sister (who held sixty-five percent of the shares), the Dutchman Jerry Blunt, and Rudy Truffino.

'Then suddenly that nut Heimadinger,' Truffino said later in an interview, 'got the idea that he didn't want to go on with Canaima, he wanted to sell his shares to Avensa.'

Formally speaking, that was impossible; the contract clearly stated that if a participant wanted to sell his shares he first had to offer them to the other shareholders. Truffino wasn't too worried about the Venezuelan sour grapes; not until he discovered that financial papers had been forged.

'Shortly after that, the German died in a very peculiar accident.'

As it turned out, the brake lines of his car had been cut.

His sister disappeared immediately afterwards; she turned up only months later, in France. Jerry Blunt was satisfied with the money he'd been offered – until far into the 1980s, you could still find him hanging around the bar of the new hotel in Canaima. Truffino packed his things, went upstream and settled in at Ucaima.

After four years of hard labour – he had often worked twenty-hour days – he was forced to start all over again. He had already built a little hut at Ucaima, it's true, but that hut was surrounded by thick undergrowth that gradually merged with the impenetrable forest. In the end, seven buildings would stand on that plot of land, in the midst of a thousand hectares of parkland. The floors of those buildings were cement, the walls were of stone. Truffino spent thousands of hours working on his camp, until it was finally fit to receive royal visitors. There was one thing, though, that made the difference with the first years at Canaima: this time, Gerti was there to help him.

'And she picked up rocks,' I heard from José Castro, the boatsman, 'that I could never have lifted on my own.'

Just how hard it is to start something far from the civilized world only really sank in the next day, when I spent a few more hours in Truffino's library. The bookcase to the left of the door was filled entirely with the books and brochures he had used as manuals while building the camp at Ucaima. Leafing through those books, I began to get a picture of what it meant to be a pioneer.

For building the houses, Truffino made use of *The Summer Home Handbook*. Those houses also had to have running water: the water came from the river. How to filter that water was something he learned from *Rural Water Supply and Sanitation*. In order to pump up the water, he needed electricity: he ordered two generators from the capital, and built a machine room, with the help of the handbook *Electricity In the Home and On the Farm*. Those generators were too big and heavy to bring in by *curiare*; the same went for the jeeps, the tractor and the cement mixer; he had to build a road to Canaima, a road ten kilometres long, straight across the savanna, and he did so with the help of the massive *Strassenbau, Vermessungswesen und Wasserwirtschaft.* Techniques for preserving fruit and vegetables he learned from the *Manuel del Aventurero, Téchnicas de supervivencia.*

After Lily came Gaby and Sabine. The children could fall ill; he and his wife could too. The nearest doctor lived three hundred kilometres away; the *Gesundheitsführer* for the tropics and for *Wüstengebiete* could help. The nearest pharmacist lived on the Orinoco as well; with the help of the guide to *Heilpflanze*, many minor ailments could be cured; for more serious complaints, they could use *Pharmazeutische Präparate.* And when things really went wrong, he could fall back on one of the few Dutch books in his library: *Verpleegkundige lessen voor de opleiding tot het diploma B.*

The children had to learn to read, write and do arithmetic; only when they were older would they go to boarding school. Most of the textbooks were written in Spanish; they learned German from the complete works of Karl May, the 1949 edition, which Gerti had received from her father when she was a little girl.

In laying out the garden – it was to become a shady park that drove botanists to raptures – Truffino took counsel from *Flowering Trees*, or from the *Gartenbuch*, a catalogue of cut flowers, the exhaustive *Plantas de las Sabanas Llaneras* and from *Palmas Tropicales Cultivadas en Venezuela.*

As director of the Canaima National Park, Truffino depended on the *Wildlife Management Techniques Manual*, on *Wildlife Conservation*, on *Brehms Tierleben* and *Fauna descriptiva de Venezuela.* He also wrote to the directors of almost all the

American national parks, who sent him their reports and conclusions. For flora, he referred to the two volume *Flora de Venezuela* by Volkmar Vareschi, or to his complete collection of the magazine *Acta Botanica Venezuela*, to the six-volume standard work by G.C.K. Dunsterville and Leslie A. Garay *Venezuelan Orchids*, Francisco Oliva-Esteva and Julian A. Steymark's *Bromeliceaes of Venezuela*, and of course, to Von Humboldt – he owned the complete Spanish language edition. I found books about butterflies, turtles, hummingbirds, caimans, mushrooms, catfish, freshwater fish, reptiles and a vast lineup of ornithological guides and three geological handbooks. But there were also five workbooks for outboard motors and seven for radio transmitters, because the telephone only reached Ucaima in the early 1980s. Using his radio equipment, he could deal directly with Carácas and Cíudad Bolívar; the transmitter was also used to contact planes and talk them down.

At first, conditions were primitive at Ucaima. After the third major orchid expedition, in April and May of 1963 – once again, with the Dunstervilles – which found eighty hitherto unknown varieties atop the Auyán Tepui, Truffino modernized the camp. The old private house was replaced with a new one, built in Indian style. Beside the little office came a dining room and a bar; he replaced the wooden floors with cement ones and built two guesthouses with room for twenty people. His collection of reptiles, butterflies, insects, hides and Indian artifacts he moved to the building he called the 'museum'; he built ten long bookcases for his collection of books and magazines, which ultimately numbered some ten thousand works; beside the museum he also built a screening room, where he showed documentaries about the Gran Sabana at the start of every expedition, so that the members would already know a good deal about the area before departure. Finally, south of the camp he built a four-hundred-metre long runway, so he could maintain his own air connections with Puerto Ordaz and Cíudad Bolívar, and was no longer dependent on Avensa.

How he financed all this remained a riddle to me. Even if the camp had room for twenty guests, it remained largely vacant throughout the five-month rainy season. The American film crews didn't worry about spending a thousand dollars here or there; the fact that Truffino could lead them straight to the ideal locations was already a huge savings in their eyes. And, in those days, the scientists were not particularly frugal either, for their research was sponsored by wealthy institutions. But even if he charged a great deal, Truffino would still have had to cut many corners in order to put together the one million he claimed to have invested in the camp – although it remained unclear to me whether he meant a million *dollars* or a million *guilders*. Far from the bureaucratic world, he didn't have to worry much about taxes: whatever ended up in his pocket he could use to his own ends. But a million is a lot of money to have to scrape together within only a few years.

What's more, adversity was a regular visitor as well. He had just finished the modernization of Ucaima when the 1967 earthquake destroyed half of Venezuela. Only two of the buildings at his camp survived the heavy shocks.

The disaster came in the middle of the night; Gerti woke him.

According to legend, she shouted: 'Hey, the house is falling down!', to which he made his characteristic reply:

'Love, just roll over and go back to sleep. We'll take a look at it in the morning.'

I came across a different kind of book in his library as well.

Somber predictions for the future, books about the end of the world. *El Enigma de la Explosión en Sibéria.* And *Nostradamus.* And *Terror en la Luna.* And *Fin del mundo año 1999.* And a detailed report of the precise effects of an atomic explosion.

Far from the civilized world, Truffino must have worried about the future. That was also clear from the great number of newspaper clippings I found about the Cuban missile crisis, and the war in Vietnam. Of the contemporary Dutch authors, he read Harry Mulisch most; I found a worn-out copy of *Het stenen bruidsbed*, about a pilot who takes part in the bombing of Dresden, as well as *Bericht aan de rattenkoning*, about the turbulent Provo era in Amsterdam in the early 1960s.

In the year that Truffino left Europe for good, the Korean War broke out, signaling the start of the Cold War. Although I found no indication that Truffino had left for South America because of the tension between East and West, it seemed that he was concerned about a new armed conflict.

In his library I also found the collected works of Erich Kästner, as well as Nietzsche's *Also sprach Zarathustra.* The three bookcases full of hard-boiled thrillers did not attest to a particularly sunny view of the world either. For Truffino, the real jungle was far away from the forest around him, and when night fell he read about Nostradamus, or about nightmarish murders in San Francisco and Los Angeles.

Six Mormons accompanied me to Angel Falls. They had arrived the afternoon before, on a plane from Puerto Ordaz.

Gerald had spent two years flogging the Book in the slums of Valencia. His parents, along with his younger sister and a couple they knew, had come to pick him up after his missionary stint. Before returning to Salt Lake City they wanted to spend a few days enjoying 'the pure surroundings of Canaima', and they had chosen Rudy's camp to do so because he seemed like 'an ascetic' to them.

As soon as I heard that, I felt like taking them to the library to see Rudy's collection of twenty pipes: long ones, short ones, fat ones, skinny ones – one for every mood. I could also have shown them a few of the photos in which Truffino was invariably seen smoking a filter cigarette. The row of bottles behind the bar also bore little witness to a sober lifestyle; there were many things the camp lacked, but there was enough rum to last for years.

At the table they read from the Book and prayed their long-winded prayers and held each other's index fingers, which they gave regular little squeezes to show their unity. They smiled all the time, in the mushy way people do who are convinced they represent the Truth and the Light; they drank no alcohol, of course, no tea, no coffee, and they didn't smoke. Gerald, who must have been well into his twenties, looked like a fourteen-year-old boy, and every time he spoke he began blushing.

Early the next morning, before sunrise, Josef drummed on the door of my room.

'They want to go to Angel Falls. Right away. Are you coming along?'

'No, I'll wait for Truffino.'

I wanted to see the legend in real life; I wanted to hear him talk, laugh, curse, brag; I wanted to view that body, battered by forty years of jungle life, with my own eyes.

'The water's rising fast, Janito. We might be able to get to Angel Falls today, but next week it will be too late. And there are six of them, with you along we can divide the costs by seven; that will save you a lot of money, man. *And I'm going with.*'

With this last statement, his floppy ears quivered; I was no match for such strength of feeling.

Nevertheless, on the first stretch of river I was in a foul mood. It was raining; I sat on the second bench back from the bow of the *curiare*, right behind Josef, and I pulled my head down into my plastic raincoat without saying a word. I had imagined that a trip to the Devil's Valley could be many things, but not that I would be nodded to the whole way by the happy faces of missionaries and amateur missionaries.

Josef tried to relieve my suffering. 'Janito, *mira, mira*,' he cried when we went on shore for lunch across from Orchid Island, 'a *martin de pescador*.' A blue-black kingfisher was buzzing the water's surface. A little later he showed me the *oro pendula*, a little brown and black bird with a yellow stripe that weaves long, hanging nests beneath tree branches. Swaying in the wind, those nests do, indeed, resemble a clock's pendulum.

After Orchid Island, the Río Carrao made a ninety-degree turn to the north and moved away from the Auyán Tepui; ten kilometres upstream we entered the Río Churún, and slowly approached the mesa. During the dry season the Churún is nothing more than a mountain stream; now, at the start of the rainy season, it had already grown twice as wide and three times as wild. The countless rapids caused us hours of delay; there was no way we would be able to reach Angel Falls the same day, the way the Mormons had hoped. They were, after all, Americans, and hurrying was second nature to them.

Out on the river they seemed all right. They helped to pull the boat over the rocks at every rapid; when things got too dangerous José Castro and his helper Juan did the work, but the Mormons carried the baggage, the cans and the boxes of supplies along the bank. Josef asked worriedly whether it wasn't too heavy for them.

'Their ancestors,' I reassured him, 'travelled two thousand kilometres to find a saltwater lake in northwestern Utah, so they're used to rolling up their sleeves. And they lead a healthy life, Josef, extremely healthy.'

'That's exactly it,' he mumbled. 'I just heard that they're teetotalers, and those coolers they're carrying so dutifully are full of beer.'

The rapids grew rougher; the drop from Angel Falls to Ucaima is four hundred and fifty metres, over a distance of a hundred and twenty kilometres; at some spots we could actually see that we were climbing up the river. The boat zigzagged back and forth. Sometimes we moved close to the bank, where the current was weakest; then we crossed at an angle to avoid an invisible ledge just beneath the water's surface. My respect for the boatsmen grew by the minute; the bowsman needed only nod to Josef, who was running the outboard, to show him where to speed up and where to go hard about; he kept his eyes fixed on the river all the time, and with water so dark he could only use the trails of rivulets to locate banks of stone sharp enough to tear open the bottom of the *curiare*. Staring for hours like that demanded the utmost concentration; that was why Truffino had always forbidden the Indians to drink alcohol during the expeditions. Josef said he was very strict about that, but then Josef himself ignored a great deal in order to keep the boatsmen happy. He had little authority over José and Juan, who clearly saw him as a greenhorn, and at the rare moments when he did give orders out on the river, Castro ignored him. Before long he had his nose buried in the Japanese textbook Truffino had given him, for señor Rudy had said that someday many Japanese tourists would come to the Gran Sabana. 'Mark my words, Josef,' he'd said. 'They're as crazy about nature as the Venezuelans are about sex.'

Late in the afternoon we pulled the *curiare* up onto a sandy beach near the foot of the Wei Tepui. It was the first stretch of sand we'd come across on our way up the Churún; the rest of the way the jungle had crept all the way down to the river's edge. We put up a tent and hung the hammocks in the trees – Truffino had once had a hut here, but it had been washed away at one point when the river had left its banks and turned into a giant whirlpool. Although the rain had stopped earlier in the day, our clothing was still soaked from the boat's spray; we hung them to dry in the last rays of sunlight and put on other clothes. The Mormons, it seemed, were not particularly prudish; had I wished I could have feasted my eyes on the women's broad hips, but I did not wish, afraid they would greet my burning glances with yet more happy smiles.

To keep the snakes and scorpions at bay we built a big fire, and roasted three chickens on it. The evening sky was aglow; dozens of hummingbirds flew around us; they were drawn by the white *bonnetia* blossoms and the reddish-purple clusters of the *thibaudia* growing among the trees, and their wings moved so quickly that they actually made a buzzing sound. José and Juan wasted no time knocking back the available cans of Polar; Josef and I did our best to keep up with them.

Night had barely fallen when the Mormons went to their hammocks; the four of us remained seated around the fire. Already quite drunk, José began cleaning his rifle; I moved out of his way a bit, but not far enough to miss out on his waking dreams of tapirs. 'The tastiest wild animal of all,' he said, smacking his lips. And immediately afterwards, in a whisper: 'But we're not allowed to shoot them anymore, we can't shoot them. Señor Rudy has forbidden it.'

After the seventh can of beer, I went to my hammock.

'Sleep in it crossways,' Josef advised me. 'If you lie in a hammock the long way, you'll hurt your back.'

Once I was lying down, he came to cover me with a mosquito net. He was giggling strangely, which might have been from the rum; after the Polar, the Pemón had moved on to the hard stuff.

'If you have to take a leak from all that beer, just stick Old Jones out of the hammock. Don't get out, there are ants here that can put you in a twenty-four hour coma.'

I thought I wouldn't be able to sleep a wink, and was awakened by the first rays of sunlight.

The Mormons had already washed in the river and were sitting on the bank, in a circle, their fingers intertwined.

'Jesus-Christ-on-a-fucking-bicycle,' said a voice behind me.

It was an expression Josef had learned from Rudy, who said it whenever someone got on his nerves. That morning I started liking Truffino even more, and thought I had even heard his voice.

We ate the leftover rice from the night before. The Mormons and I ate with forks; José, Juan and Josef used flat pieces of manioc biscuit.

'The food of nomads,' José said.

Preparing manioc is a long and complicated process; the deadly poisonous prussic acid must first be pressed from the roots of the cassava. But when baked, the manioc biscuits stay good for weeks.

We struck out early onto a river that was growing wilder all the time. At the first set of rapids the *curiare* hit a big, flat stone, spun ninety degrees and became a powerless matchstick in the grip of the current. A second stone kept the boat from making a full turn, which would surely have capsized us; Josef used his paddle to push off with all his might, and the *curiare* righted itself again.

'Start bailing!' he shouted. It turned out to be the best way to recover from our fright. Using tin cans, we bailed the water out of the boat. Later, kilometres further upriver, I was suddenly reminded of Simon Schama's words in his essay about Sir Walter Raleigh in *Landscape and Memory*: 'And what the discoverers immediately discover is that they cannot control the river. The river controls them.'

Raleigh had set sail for Venezuela in the greedy grip of the myth of El Dorado. Schama typifies that myth as 'a jumble of fables that confounded Ovid's lost Golden Age with Inca gold.' The discovery that the Indians along the Río Caroní wore golden jewellery, and that they were willing to trade some of those pieces, struck the Europeans blind with avarice. In every rumour they heard proof that the kingdom of gold really existed, the vaguest of nods confirmed their belief that it must lie south of the Orinoco. The Spaniards were the first to enter the interior, followed by Germans in the service of the Welsers' banking house. In their wake, Sir Walter Raleigh sailed up the Orinoco in April of 1595. 'And every stone we picked up,' he wrote in his journal, 'held the promise of silver or gold.' But, just like the Spanish colonel Antonio de Berrio, he never succeeded in penetrating the area and finding the city of Manoa, upstream along the Caroní. Legend had it that Dorado lay not far from there, on the shores of Lake Pariame, and the Indians had told Berrio that that the clear water of that lake twinkled with gold and silver stones, like a reflection of the night sky. During the 17th century, Lake Pariame appeared on many European maps, just a little north of present-day Canaima.

In the 18th century, when the lake was discovered to be mythical, the interest in southeastern Venezuela declined. From time to time, however, gold fever would flare up again and a few hundred desperados would hurry to the Guyanese highlands to be devoured by the anacondas and jaguars, or to die of mysterious illnesses.

Under the Treaty of Munster, Spain and the Republic of the Netherlands had established a number of vague agreements about their only common border: the one in Guyana. What was later to become British Guiana (the colonies of Essequibo, Demerara and Berbice) was at that time in the hands of the Dutch, while Venezuela was part of Spain's empire. In the 19th century, there was still no clarity about the border; Venezuela, which had by then gained independence from Spain, laid claim to a large part of the eastern territory. And after the British left Guiana in 1966, the conflict smoldered on; even today, an enormous area east of the Gran Sabana is marked on every Venezuelan map as *Zona en reclamación con Guyana*.

The first to catch a glimpse of the Gran Sabana were the German brothers Richard and Robert Schomburgk, biologists contracted by the British crown to explore the area between Guiana and Venezuela. They left home in 1835, and after years of travel reached the slopes of the Roraima, the easternmost *tepui* marking the border between Venezuela, Brazil and Guiana. Robert Schomburgk began the climb, but had to give up quite quickly: the walls of the Roraima are as steep and rugged as those of the Auyán Tepui. The first route to the top was found in 1884 by an English biologist with a German name, Everard F. Im Thurn, and his companion, Harry I. Perkins. Their expedition was also financed by the British Royal Geographical Society.

By charting the area as thoroughly as possible and encouraging scientific publication, the British hoped firmly to entrench their claim to it. The Venezuelans, on the other hand, were conspicuous by their absence. Venezuelan historians later assembled an impressive list of retired military men and superannuated adventurers who had supposedly explored the Gran Sabana from the late 19th century on; none of them, however, had put their findings on paper. None, that is, but Juan María Mundó Freixas, and he would have done better not to. He is the one responsible for the name 'La Gran Sabana', with which he created more confusion than clarity. Mundo published his travelogue in 1929 in the magazine *Cultura Venezolana*; it was not until 1932 that he caught a glimpse of the Sarisariñama, and in 1937 of the Auyán Tepui, and by then he too was disappointed with himself for having given the area a name that suggested a huge prairie.

The first Venezuelan to explore in any serious fashion was Felix Cardona Puig. In 1936 he climbed the south face of the Auyán Tepui; if he had walked on, he would have come to the

Rudy and Gerti Truffino with their daughters Lily, Gaby and Sabine
(photo: R. Truffino archives)

Rudy Truffino, c.1968 (photo: H. Truffino archives)

Charlie Baughan amid the Pemón Indians (photo from Ruth
Robertson's *Churún Méru – The Tallest Angel*)

The non-venomous coral snake (photo: R. Truffino)

Two Pemón women, Canaima, 1957 (photo: G. Koppenwallner)

Pemón hunters with blowgun, Canaima, 1957
(photo: G. Koppenwallner)

At the *conuco*, 1957 (photo: G. Koppenwallner)

Gerti Koppenwallner, during her second visit to Canaima, 1958
(photo: R. Truffino archives)

Ruth Robertson (l.), standing beside Aleksander Laime
(photo from Ruth Robertson's *Churún Méru – The Tallest Angel*)

Aleksander Laime's hut at the foot of the Auyán Tepui
(photo: J. Brokken)

Rudy Truffino on expedition with a Venezuelan film crew
(photo: R. Truffino archives)

Rudy Truffino on the Auyán Tepui, 1960
(photo: R. Truffino archives)

highest waterfall in the world, but he turned back and left that honour to Jimmy Angel, who crashed there one year later. In fact, when Angel came back with his sensational news, the reaction in Carácas was largely one of disbelief.

Venezuela's lack of enthusiasm is perhaps not so surprising. Their 19th century was a chaotic one; in the early 20th century they fixed their attention on extracting oil from Lake Maracaibo. The next area they developed lay just behind the Orinoco delta, where inexhaustible deposits of iron ore lay just below the surface. Beside the steel mills, a whole new city was built, Cíudad Guayana; seventy kilometres to the south arose the enormous Guria Dam for the catchment of water from the Río Caroni. The authorities left the study of plants and animals to foreigners; to the American ornithologist William Phelps, and to his son William Jr. and his wife Kathleen Deery de Phelps, who explored the south side of the Auyán Tepui, the Autana, the Yavi, the Parú and the Sierra de la Neblina during the period 1937-1967. There was also Dunsterville, who was attached to Harvard University, and Steyermark, whose expeditions were funded by the Botanical Garden of Missouri, as well as Bassett Maguire, who carried out his studies on behalf of the New York Botanical Garden. Due to the pioneering work of Laime and Truffino, and the pilots Angel and Baughan, they were able to reach the tops of the mesas and return with huge quantities of data. Maguire collected more than ten thousand varieties of plants, Steyermark more than twenty-seven thousand. As thanks for their efforts, their names were sometimes put on the map; one of the summits of the Mountains in the Mist received the name Pico Phelps; a set of rapids below Canaima was named after Rudy Truffino, the Salto Rudy (bastardized by the Indians into Salto Yudi or Yuri) and, of course, there is the Salto Angel.

The story behind Jimmy Angel's arrival in Venezuela is a wonderful one, not a single word of which can be verified today. Angel related his exploits to L.R. Dennison, who published them as *Devil Mountain*. I found a copy in Truffino's library; the margins were crawling with notes. A description of the falls Truffino had annotated with the word 'NUTS!!!' The walls of the canyon, Dennison said, were 'pure white'. Truffino corrects him: 'brown and black.' According to Dennison, there is nothing edible to be found in the valley, Truffino recommends that he try '*pescado*'; there are, Dennison says, almost no animals in the canyon, and again Truffino corrects him: 'Tapir. Jaguar. Puma.'

Jimmy Angel was flat broke when an old Mexican mining engineer approached him in the lobby of a hotel in Panama and offered him five thousand dollars to fly him in his Flamingo to a mesa in an uncharted part of Venezuela's Gran Sabana. According to Dennison, that meeting took place in 1923. Ruth Robertson offers another version, which she bases on an article by Thomas Guillard in *The Saturday Evening Post*. Guillard said the meeting took place in 1921 in a bar in Panama, and in his version the old mining engineer was a seasoned gold digger from Alaska, Mr. McCracken. He offered not five, but three thousand dollars, still an astronomical sum in those days. Angel flew the man to the Auyán Tepui and succeeded in landing his Flamingo on a little strip of ground, a hellish task in the forceful downdrafts. Close to a little river they began to dig in the gravel, and within three days they collected seventy-five pounds of gold. Had the single-prop Flamingo been able to lift much more than that, they would have taken more. The gold was sold for twelve thousand dollars.

That was why Angel was determined to find that spot again

at any cost. He flew south from Cíudad Bolivar on numerous occasions. To ensure himself of the proper permits, he took the sons of dictator Juan Vincente Gómez with him, both of whom had also contracted gold fever.

James Crawford Angel was a true virtuoso at the joystick. He was barely eighteen when he flew his first mission above Germany and the trenches of France for the Canadian Royal Air Force. In the 1920s he had earned his keep as a stunt flyer in the United States, in the thirties he worked as a flight instructor for Sun Yat-sen's air force in China. Back in his home country, he performed the most dangerous stunt dives in Howard Hughes's film *Hell Angels*; after that he headed down to Central and South America, where he hired out his services as a bush pilot.

Before landing on the Auyán Tepui again, he made a few flights to the Gran Sabana with the wealthy American engineer Curry. The American was prepared to pay a great deal in order to have his name associated with an area as yet uncharted; when he climbed out of the plane deep in the bush, he was bitten by a snake and died.

In 1935 Angel followed the course of the Río Churún, flew past an enormous rock wall and saw the gigantic waterfall that would bear his name. A mile high, he estimated.

Two years later he flew into the Devil's Valley once more, along with his wife Marie and the geologist Gustavo Heny, who had brought along his gardener to do the heavier digging. Heny had already explored the south side of the Auyán Tepui; the other reason why Angel granted him a seat in his plane and promised him a share of the booty was that Heny was only truly in his element when he had lost his way deep in the jungle.

He showed Heny 'his' waterfall, circled the top of the

Auyán Tepui three times and thought he recognized the spot
where he had once landed. This time his landing was a bit
sloppier; one wheel sank into the peaty soil and the left wing
was wrecked. That broken wing meant there was no way to
take off again. The impact when the plane hit had also
knocked loose the instrument panel, and the radio was out.
No matter how he tried, Angel was unable to transmit a
distress signal.

Now that the four of them were atop the mighty
mountain, the question was how they would ever get down
again. Heny suggested they walk to the south face. They sank
to their knees in swamps, clambered over ledges, and eleven
days later reached the rock wall that would later be given the
name 'Second Wall'. With a rope they had found in the
Flamingo's emergency kit, they scaled their way down to the
rocky plateau. At that point they were still a thousand metres
above the valley floor.

By sheer luck, Heny found the path he had discovered in
1936 when he climbed the south side of the *tepui* with Felix
Cardona Puig and Miguel Delgado. They arrived at the
bottom weak with hunger. They walked along a river for a
day; then they heard the regular slap of paddles in the water
and saw a couple of Indians. The Indians took them to the
mission post at Camarata, where they were able to call in a
plane on the shortwave radio.

Back in Carácas, Angel told his story to anyone who would
listen. Discovery, however, is one thing; being believed is
another. There were already countless legends told about the
mysterious south. In addition, Angel had a trait one is better
off not having when when one has a great announcement to
make: an exceptionally big mouth. It took twenty years before
he received anything like the acknowledgement he deserved.

On one of his trips to the top of the Auyán Tepui, Aleksander Laime found Angel's plane. He pulled out the radio, found a few snake skins behind the instrument panel, and unscrewed the metal plate on the fuselage that bore the name of the plane: El Río Caroní. Truffino also succeeded in finding the plane. When he came by it for the eighth time, during the 1963 orchid expedition, it was still in good shape; the aluminum glistened, and even the two red stripes on the fuselage were still unfaded. In August of 1965, Truffino led Angel's seventeen-year-old son Rolan and two reporters from *Life* magazine to the wreck. They placed a memorial beside the plane. Five years later, helicopters brought the wreckage down piece-by-piece, and the plane received a place of honour in front of the airport at Cíudad Bolívar, as final proof of Angel's daring. A replica of the plane was installed on the Auyán Tepui.

The media attention given to the search for Angel's plane unleashed a new wave of gold fever. In December of 1964, a Cessna took off from Canaima; twenty-four hours later, it was reported missing. A military aircraft located the plane on top of the Auyán Tepui; the two American pilots were digging for gold. In February of 1965, two other American pilots ran out of fuel and made an emergency landing on the Auyán Tepui. Like Angel, they had to walk down the mountain and arrived more dead than alive at Camarata, where they were immediately arrested for illegal trading in gold and diamonds. The news was splashed across the papers in fat black headlines; Truffino never missed a single article, and cut them all out. The Auyán Tepui had clearly become his mountain, and perhaps he hoped to someday make a find there that would relieve him of all his financial cares.

Jimmy Angel himself continued to dream of gold for the

rest of his life. In the late 1940s, he confided in Ruth Robertson that he had found El Dorado.

'It was during a storm,' he said, 'and Marie and I looked down and saw a city on an island under the surface of the lake. We could see the walls and the streets through the holes in the clouds. Then it disappeared, and we never saw it again.'

Where was it he had seen that city?

'Somewhere in the green jungle.'

In addition to dreaming, he also kept on drinking. In 1956, while in Panama, he climbed into his plane in a state of complete intoxication. During the flight he noticed nothing; when he climbed out, his legs felt like lead. He walked a few hundred metres, then collapsed on the street, once and for all.

The water fell past grey-red-white rocks. The forest crowded in on itself to get closer to the water; it climbed up over the rocks, tumbled over the steepest crags. Impossible for trees to grow on rock; yet here they did, thanks to the spray of water from above.

Salto Angel does not thunder or clatter. The fall is too great for that; before the water has even touched the ground, it has nebulized into huge clouds. The sound the waterfall makes is that of a constant, gentle spring shower.

Not far from where Salto Angel sprays the treetops, along a bank of the Churún, Truffino had cleared a patch of forest and used river stones to build a lodge. A simple building, with a fireplace against the back wall to keep warm on cool evenings and a room with eight bunkbeds.

It was too late to start climbing; besides, there was rain in the air again and the path looked dangerously slippery. José predicted that we would wouldn't be able to go up the next day either, but that didn't seem to bother him much. He was

Pémon enough to fear the mountain; after a furtive tug at the bottle of rum, he curled up in his hammock. To the east and west of the waterfall, in any event, there was no way to reach the top of the mesa; after a few hundred metres the path came to a dead end. From the highest point of the climb you could see the entire canyon, and the panorama alone, it seems, was worth the blisters and the exhaustion.

Wading through water so clear we could see the pebbles glistening on the bottom, Josef and I crossed the river and walked into the canyon which grew more narrow with each passing kilometre. 'We're going to take a shower under the waterfall,' he said to the others, but although the spray caressed our backs the whole way, the real reason must have been a different one. I had the impression Josef wanted to tell me something; he had left the boatsman lying in the hammock and had turned down Juan's offer to go with us. We were only off for a little walk, he'd said, but we followed the river for hours. At first I thought he wanted to look for medicinal plants and seeds; a little later, after clearing his throat hesitantly, he started in on a story of which I couldn't make head or tail. On the way back, an approaching thunderstorm made him hurry; the rumbling in the valley was growing increasingly ominous.

Back at the hut I changed into dry clothes for the third time that day. I barely had them on before they started feeling clammy again. Only in front of the fire José and Juan had built did the dampness, which I had carried around all day like a cold, begin to dry up.

We ate at the long, rough-hewn table in front of the fireplace. Halfway through the meal my shoe made contact with something which I first thought was the foot of the lady next to me. I didn't immediately suspect any ulterior motive, let alone the slightly clumsy onset of a flirtation, although the rumour about the pious is that they are strict of doctrine and loose of morals; nonetheless, I kept feeling something, and finally looked under the table. The round, dark thing that lay there aroused my suspicion, perhaps because it was so motionless, right in front of my shoe. I pointed it out to Josef.

He shouted: 'A bushmaster!'

The Indians were the first ones up onto the benches, the Mormons and I followed a hundredth of a second later. Josef grabbed a fork, bent back the two teeth in the middle and suddenly threw himself on the table, knocking a pan, a couple of knives and a plate to the floor. This caused the snake to awaken from its peaceful slumber; it shot forward, and at the same moment Josef leaned down and jammed the fork into its body, right behind the head, with both hands. The bushmaster wriggled three times and was dead.

Josef carried the snake outside, still dangling from the fork. José and Juan didn't move; I had to grab the flashlight to light Josef's way. A little ways from the lodge he laid the bushmaster on a flat stone, by the river.

'I'll skin it tomorrow.'

When we got back to the hut, the Mormons had folded their hands again and were listening to Gerald's prayer, fiery as that of an apostle. José and Juan were talking right through it all with equal fervor, both nursing a bottle of rum. I sought my own respite in the supply of Polar, and after each can I slapped Josef on the shoulder just a little harder. He simply scratched his head, amazed at so much elation; that evening we may have seen him as our hero, but he remained the skinny kid who laughed nervously now and then to disguise his shyness.

The next morning he stripped the skin off the metre-and-a-half-long snake and stuffed it into a glass jar. He figured someone might pay a pretty penny for it, back in Ciudad Bolívar.

It was raining so hard that Salto Angel had dissolved in the downpour; the water was coming off the mountain in waves. Even for an experienced mountain climber, the journey up the rock wall would have been a risky one; no one felt like breaking an arm or a leg in the middle of the wilderness. The Mormons whined that couldn't stay any longer; to demonstrate just how much of a hurry they were in, they went and sat in the *curiare*, wearing their backpacks for good measure. We could have shoved off right away had the boatsman and the bowsman taken their places, but they had disappeared into the woods without saying where they were going.

Josef went off looking for them. When the three of them returned, they were all avoiding each other's glance. It was the snakeskin, I realized; the Indians didn't want Josef to take it with him in the boat. He might speak of himself as a Pemón, but to José and Juan he belonged to the city, and anyone who hadn't grown up in the forest didn't know the power of the *canaima*.

It took a lot of talking on their part before Josef consented to leave the skin behind. But that wasn't enough for José and Juan. Josef had to build a fire, as far from the hut as possible, and throw the snakeskin into the flames, along with the glass jar. Then he had to undress and cleanse himself in the river.

He did so expressionlessly, wearing only his underpants.

After the ritual was over, we could start the journey home.

Going with the current went twice as fast. We reached Ucaima that same day. Instead of eating dinner, I took a shower and crawled into bed. The next morning I found a present in front of my door; the Latter Day Saints, who had taken the first plane out, had left me their Book. After breakfast I put it on a shelf in the library, and spent the rest of the morning pouring over Dunsterville's account of his trip with Truffino to the Auyán Tepui.

'Thick clouds had gathered to the north, east and south. There was a distant clap of thunder and a few drops fell from the sky. A storm was clearly on its way. Rudy cast a glance at the two tents we had sent up the night before on the dry river bed, and regretfully suggested we move camp to higher ground in the forest. To be awakened by a fast-rising river might present some inconveniences; for his wife Gerti, it would also be rather confusing to see us come floating past her door the next day, a full two weeks before she expected us back.'

My enthusiasm about travelling with Truffino was boosted again, and I decided to stay a few more days at Ucaima.

Under the motto 'better safe than sorry', Truffino and Dunsterville had taken every possible precaution. Both of them had a supply of antivenom in their pack; both of them were carrying bright yellow cloths they could spread out on open ground in an emergency, to draw the attention of the bush pilot who would fly over on the seventh or eighth day of the expedition. But when they finally heard the plane, they were busy slashing a trail through thick brush, and the pilot saw only the ten bearers walking out in front, without yellow cloths. On treks like those it was impossible to foresee all eventualities, and they remained dangerous, no matter how well Truffino knew the surroundings. He'd had to cut short the first trip with Dunsterville after only seven days, because of bad weather. But during those seven days the orchid specialist had seen enough to make him want to return as soon as possible; on the next trip, he brought his wife along. At home in Carácas, as he arranged the orchids he'd collected, Dunsterville sighed: 'Long before I am settled, I shall be off again.'

Rummaging through some old detergent boxes, I found even more clippings. In 1963, *National Geographic* had sent a team to Ucaima. In 1968, *The Pittsburgh Journal* had sponsored an expedition by the Pittsburgh Explorers Club, and published six articles about it. A German scientific journal described the expedition by the Bayerische Botanische Gesellschaft.

For a full twenty years, Truffino spent much of his time accompanying naturalists who were eager to make use of his encyclopaedic knowledge. He led the bromeliad specialist to the rarest specimen, the orchid collector to a valley where thousands grew, and each morning he took the authority on caymans to a sandbank on a little river, high above the rapids, where he could spend the whole day coming to grips with the object of his study. Afterwards they sent Truffino their reports, with a dedication or a word of thanks. It must have been a satisfying period for him; others could demonstrate the scientific importance of their findings, and he had been the one who helped them to get started.

In 1974, the Von Humboldt Foundation invited him to give a lecture in Carácas to an audience consisting largely of botanists. He spent months preparing for that evening. What he finally presented, the newpapers reported, was a passionate and minutely documented plea for the preservation of the Gran Sabana.

Interest in his pioneering work was growing outside Venezuela as well. Beneath Dunsterville's report I found a few letters from an American journalist who wanted to publish Truffino's lifestory in book form. The fact that the request was repeated a number of times led me to conclude that Truffino had never sent the man a reply.

Truffino and the Venezuelan painter Lopez Mendes used to listen to Mozart together. Lopez Mendes returned to Ucaima every year, in search of divine skyscapes, which he used again and again as background for the big canvases he painted with such Expressionistic verve. But as soon as darkness fell, he and his host would sit down to *Don Giovanni*.

Truffino told the painter that he had acquired his love of music right after the war, in the days when all young Europeans came to associate their newly won freedom with jazz. But once in Ucaima he had started listening to the records Gerti had brought with her from Austria, and had discovered that Mozart was much better music for the jungle. Evenings tended to be long out in the bush, especially during the rainy season; at such times, the feeling of desolation lay crouched like a ravenous beast, and unless you were careful it would fly at you and drag you to the abyss, where a bottomless emptiness stared you in the face, the same emptiness Kurtz must have seen in *The Heart of Darkness* when he murmured 'the horror, the horror'. Duke Ellington could chase that feeling away, and when he listened to Ella Fitzgerald he felt like embracing all the women in the world, but the sense that life was too sweet to let it be sullied by despondency was something he experienced best when humming along with 'Madamina'.

With David Leach, an Englishman and one of the world's most famous ceramists, he listened to Mozart just as often. Leach, too, came back to Ucaima each year. Truffino would reserve the entire camp for him if he could, so they could do some catching up or simply enjoy the silence, with Mozart as the only high volume intermezzo. And when they had listened all the way through the final act of *Don Giovanni*, Truffino would say what he said to everyone: 'Mozart chases away the heartbreak.'

Heartbreak?

In Boeli van Leeuwen's novel *The Stumbling Block*, Truffino had underlined the following sentences:

'Can a person flee from himself? Is there a continent distant enough that heartbreak will not follow him, new enough that his footprints will blow away in the wind and be erased? The earth is round, and on a globe roads have no end; why shouldn't I catch up with my own shadow, again and again? [...] I wanted to go to a continent where life was reduced to its essential parts; heaven and earth and, between them, Man, held upright by the hinges of his own joints. I waxed homesick for the silence of the desert and the mystery of the jungle. In the alleys of Europe I could not find the truth; in the cathedrals I was alone with my despair. And so I left for Venezuela, the land where, under the rocks around the Ilano, the scorpions sleep with their stingers curled on their backs.'

Not a story or article about the Gran Sabana appeared in those years without Truffino in it. Venezuelan state television made a documentary about Ucaima. He was referred to with increasing frequency as a 'living legend', and that attracted the attention of the highborn and the famous.

I rummaged through the boxes of photos and picked out Britain's Princess Margaret, her nephew Prince Charles, Farah Diba, the three children of the Spanish King Juan Carlos, Canadian prime minister Trudeau, David Rockefeller, Neil

Armstrong, the Venezuelan Miss Universe Irene Sáez – who would later become mayor of a Carácas suburb and later still take a stab at the presidency – and a man whose face I did not recognize, but who had written on the back of the photo that he was the great-great-great-grandson of Christopher Columbus. And they had all had their picture taken with Rudy, or with his three towheaded daughters.

Most of those pictures were now stuck together; the colours faded, the edges stained brown with moisture. The boxes they were kept in were covered in a thick layer of dust; when I picked up one of them, a battalion of ants went scurrying off. Spiders and cockroaches had nested amid the faces, and apparently had no intention of ever leaving again. In some of the boxes they had left behind a trail of slime; the mortality stuck to my fingers.

The first jet to arrive at Canaima landed on January 24th, 1975, on a runaway that had by then been paved. At the joystick was the Dutch prince consort. Prince Bernhard was accompanied by his aide-de-camp, his personal secretary, the Dutch ambassador to Venezuela, the Venezuelan ambassador to the Netherlands, two pilots and the inevitable royalty reporter on the Dutch daily *De Telegraaf*, Stan Huygens. Huygens had not been invited to visit Ucaima, and had to remain at Canaima.

Bernhard was immediately impressed by Truffino. 'What that man has achieved in the jungle,' he told Stan Huygens two days later, 'borders on the impossible.'

Truffino, on the other hand, found his royal highness a bit taxing. 'He just kept jabbering away,' he told his friends from Curaçao, 'about how young he looked for his age and how old I looked for mine. At a certain point I got fed up. I said to him: 'Stop. Holland is just some shitty little country, but how many people do you need to run it? This park here covers thirty thousand square kilometres, and I run it on my own.' Bernhard looked sort of horrified for a moment, then took the pipe out of his mouth and laughed that little hiccupping laugh of his. He had to admit: I had him there.'

His dealings with Prince Charles were much more formal. The Prince of Wales communicated his wishes and whims to Truffino in writing, in the form of notes delivered by his private secretary.

Two months after the royal entourage had left, Truffino received a letter from squadron leader D.J. Checketts, which he put in with the pictures of Prince Charles.

Dear Rudi,

The Prince of Wales has asked me to write and let you know how very much he enjoyed his all too brief stay at your camp near Canaima.

His Royal Highness thoroughly enjoyed every moment and was only sorry that he was unable to stay longer. However, His Royal Highness is determined that he will return one day to enjoy your fantastic hospitality.

His Royal Highness sends his very sincere thanks and appreciation to you, your family, and your assistants, to which I would like to add the thanks of everyone in the Royal Party for being made so comfortable and welcome.

I put down the letter and stared for a while at the albino peacocks Truffino had brought in from Europe, which were parading across the lawn between the library and the river, until a pair of chattering toucans came and chased them away.

Truffino enlarged the photos himself. In his little shed, behind the water tank, the generator room and the hangar, he had fixed up a complete darkroom. Sometimes at night I would see light coming from that building, strange light; the light of a lamp or an oil lantern, swaying softly in the wind.

He made contact prints of all the pictures he took; I found piles of them, of birds, snakes, flowers, clouds, turtles, and of his daughters. I saw the girls grow up. Their skirts grew shorter, their breasts bigger. The swimming suits turned into bikinis, the bikini bottoms into strings. Lily was always the most provocative, with her muscular arms, muscular legs, muscular buttocks and muscular stomach. With Gaby, it was the face full of freckles that was photographed most, and with Sabine it was the straight blonde hair blowing back from her long neck. As children, the photos often showed them playing naked among their Indian contemporaries; later they are seen in skimpy dresses, standing among the guests.

The photos I held in my hand longest were the ones Truffino had made during his trip to visit the Yanomami. Glossy colour prints, 24x24. There was no way for me to tell precisely when he had canoed up the Orinoco; I suspected it was somewhere in the late 1970s. Perhaps it was Jacques Lizot who had whetted his appetite for the Amazon; Lizot's book appeared in 1976, and in Truffino's library I found the Spanish translation, *El Círculo de los Fuegos, Vida y costumbres de los indios Yonomami*, which came out in 1978. One thing is certain: he made the trip alone. None of the photos showed a travelling companion.

He also went to Kenya on his own, with a bag full of bird, animal and plant guides. I didn't think twice about it at the time; it seemed clear to me that one could not leave a jungle camp behind unmanned, and that one of the Truffinos would remain behind while the other took care of business in the capital, or went off to catch their breath from the hectic life at

Ucaima – there were always guests at the table, Sundays and holidays included, and those guests wanted to be entertained. Gerti went to Guadeloupe or Martinique to relax, while Rudy made increasingly longer journeys on his own, and that was all.

Upon his return from Africa he built a round hut, right down beside the river, with a view of the Kurawaina Tepui, the Kurasari and, in the distance, the northern flank of the Auyán Tepui. The hut had no walls or windows, you could feel every breeze there, it had only four chairs and a chimney of quartz; there was something unmistakably British about it, he must have come up with the idea while visiting a similar building, perhaps with a view of Kilimanjaro.

Late that afternoon, I went down there. The chairs had not been dusted in months, the walls badly needed painting.

The longer I stayed at Ucaima, the more I noticed how the camp was decaying. It was as though no one looked after it anymore, despite all the years of hard work.

The last touches of red had left the sky. The clouds slid before the mountains like a curtain. While I watched the fog settle down just over the savanna, I wondered who the women were who I'd come across in the bottommost box of contact prints. Women in their thirties or forties, baring their breasts to the camera just a little too frivolously, or posing without any clothing at all, beneath a waterfall, hands clasped behind their heads or running their fingers through their long, wet hair, standing on one leg with a hand on one hip, or held a little lower, fingers stretched coyly in front of the glistening hairs at their crotch. Rudy's girlfriends? Conquests from around the campfire during a long trek? Or were these the wives of businessmen and diplomats who, in the freedom of the wilds, had let themselves go completely before having to wriggle back into their matched suits? They were all smiling in any event, some more nervously than others.

The nude models sent by the German weekly *Neue Revue* have a much cooler bearing. They lean on Rudy's shoulder, or grasp his hand to keep from slipping beneath the Sapo waterfall, or gallop across the savanna with him on horseback, in the nude. He always remains dressed, never even taking off his felt hat. Oh well, he must have thought, it pays well enough, times are tough all over, *la noche post petrolera* has fallen, everyone in the country is suffering from double-digit inflation, so... But still, in those photos he looks rather sad. The days when every step he took brought him closer to the unknown were past by then, the discoveries had been made, the scientists flew to the mesas by helicopter. And now, old before his time, skinnier than ever, there we have him with Rita and Brigitta, meant to bring something like a rumble of lust to the churning Bavarian beer belly.

Yet another film crew came to Ucaima to make a movie, but this time the actors and actresses performed under pseudonyms. The film was *Emmanuelle VI*. The leading role was played by a German fashion model; in the movie, she runs afoul of an Indian woman from the Amazon. The role of the Indian woman was played by a Spanish-Moroccan actress. The German girl could have passed for a life-sized Barbie doll; the pseudo-Indian was a ravishing beauty. Truffino must have seen that too; in the picture where he lays his hand on the desirable hip of the Amazon he looks a little more cheerful, but his cheekbones are gaunt beneath his wrinkled skin and his stubbly beard has gone grey.

Like every morning, the Indian girl was combing her hair imperturbably, sitting on the flat rock in the first rays of sunlight right before my room.

I opened Charles Brewer-Carías' work on the vegetation of the *Mundo Perdido*, with lots of nice illustrations for reading in the hammock, and looked at her. Finally, after all those days, her gaze met mine. I stood up, discovered that my leg was asleep, limped over to her and asked whether she was señor Rudy's girlfriend.

She shook her head.

'No, señor Armando's.'

'And who is señor Armando?'

'Sabine's husband.'

Truffino's son-in-law, married to his youngest daughter.

'And where is Sabine?'

'In Carácas. She doesn't come here much anymore…'

She smiled at me and tied her hair back with a red ribbon.

It was raining once more; we had to wrap ourselves in plastic again. We took the dugout a few kilometres upriver, changed to the truck, drove past the airstrip and then continued north by canoe until we got to the Yudi or Yuri rapids, named after Rudy, because he was the first white man to have crossed them the time the old Indian brought him to Lola Castro. Here was where it had all started; his knowledge of the Indians and their ways, the journeys by river, the acquaintance with a world full of birds, snakes and spirits.

'*Mira!*' Josef shouted after we had settled down on a flat rock in the middle of the rapids. Two cockatoos flew overhead, bright blue, bright red. Their shrieks drowned out the sound of a hundred other birds. Right above the water a pair of *morphos* came gliding by, and once again I stared openmouthed at their blinding colour, bluer than the deepest royal blue.

We returned to the camp around noon. After lunch I

walked out onto the savanna, along the road Truffino had cut through the forest with his own hands, to an open field.

At the end of the grass strip was the Cessna, under its plastic tarp. I walked towards the plane. When I got close, Tièta suddenly jumped out at me.

Had it been an ocelot or a tapir, I couldn't have been more terrified. You at least know that those animals are dangerous; with a dog, you can never tell. Fond of its master and oh-so-loyal, to be sure, but I was not his master, and he had never even seen me with his master. I didn't know the words his master used to soothe him; but then Tièta, that impressive cross between a Great Dane and a St. Bernhard, didn't actually seem to me like the kind who panicked quickly. He pressed his muzzle against my chest and began pushing me back. 'Get away from that plane,' was his message, and he conveyed it without a growl or a bark. He just pushed, calm and self-assured.

He kept pushing me back, off the grass landing strip and onto the road, through the woods. By then I had turned around, and he kept following me. Whenever I'd stop for a moment, he would prod me a little; he didn't mean to be overbearing, but this was no time for dawdling.

At a certain point he bounded off to the right, to an open spot in the forest. A flat stone, a cross on top. It had to be a grave. I walked over to the stone and read: Rudolf J.M. Truffino van der Lugt (Jungle Rudy), 7-12-1928 11-1-1994.

The man I wanted to meet had already been dead for more than a year.

'**Why** didn't you tell me?'

Josef shrugged.

'You know, he'd been sick for a long time. He had cancer in his lung, in his stomach, in his knees, in his head. First he stopped going along when we went up the Auyán Tepui, then he stopped going to Angel Falls, and in the end he didn't even go along to Orchid Island. He just stayed in his house. But the guests came for Jungle Rudy, so sometimes he would show his face at the bar for half an hour, and he'd promise that the next day he would definitely go along. We got used to it, used to saying that, of course, señor Rudy would go along… tomorrow…or the next day…'

They kept doing it even after he had died; it wasn't really lying, they simply remained vague about the man who was so inextricably linked to the camp.

'Everyone wanted to see the legend, everyone wanted to hear his stories. So we said he'd gone to town or that he didn't feel well, and then, well, most of the guests left after three or four days. But you stayed, and then you started nosing around in his things. With you it was harder; I was planning to tell your earlier, but I noticed that you started liking him more all the time, and I was afraid to disappoint you.'

He shuffled over to the bar, mixed himself a *cuba libre*, took a sip of it, then mixed one for me as well. In mine, he put a double shot of rum.

'It's understandable,' I said, to make him feel a little better. 'Completely understandable.'

He shook his head angrily.

'I'm leaving, Janito. I can work my fingers to the bone here, I can organize the most fantastic trips, make the worst expeditions turn out all right, I know every tree, every plant, every bird and every mushroom; but the people aren't satisfied. They want señor Rudy.'

Indeed, it seemed to me like a hopeless cause.

It was already dusk when Josef took me to Truffino's hut. He knocked a few times. Señor Armando opened the door; so this was the man who had moved into Rudy's house, Truffino's son-in-law, the stocky man with the gold chain, the one I'd seen at the bar on a number of occasions.

Almost nothing had changed inside since Rudy died. A little room with his radio transmitter, a darkened alcove – his darkroom. In the middle of the room hung the hammock in which he had spent his final hours; on the floor lay a book, *El general en su labertino* by Gabriel García Marquez; the bookmark was at page eighty-four, he hadn't had time to finish it.

Armando, who spoke almost no English, showed me everything without comment. He opened a drawer, pointed to the hundreds of cassette tapes. Ella Fitzgerald, Duke Ellington, Louis Armstrong, Chet Baker, Lionel Hampton, Dizzy Gillespie, John Coltrane, Benny Waters, Charlie Parker, Bill Coleman. But also Fleetwood Mac, the Stones. And Bach's *Wohltemperierte Klavier* in the best rendition by far (with Sviatoslav Richter), Beethoven's string quartets, the preludes of Debussy (by Walter Gieseking, once again one of the loveliest renditions), Ravel, Bartók, Mahler and Mozart, lots of Mozart, all the symphonies, all the piano concertos, the trios, the quintets, the clarinet quartet, almost all the operas, *Don Giovanni* as conducted by Karl Böhm; the same recording I had at home, on vinyl.

Armando shoved a cassette into the player. I heard Truffino's voice, with the soft rustle of Angel Falls in the background. The kind of voice I'd thought he'd have, low, matter-of-fact, not too serious, not too sarcastic either. The recording had been made on one of his last trips, when he climbed the Auyán Tepui with a group of Americans.

I heard him laugh, I heard him pant, I heard him explaining things with his last bit of breath, I heard him cutting away saplings on the steep path up.

The next morning I left the Gran Sabana, in my ears the footsteps of an old man climbing his mountain one last time, before stretching his legs forever.

II

064 Level
042 Plumb

One year later I was back in Venezuela, to give a reading at the *Asociación Holandesa* in Carácas. I was staying at the house of the undersecretary of the Dutch embassy, in a neighbourhood cut off from the rest of the city by the kind of fence one sees around prisons, in a house whose wrought iron grillwork at the windows and doors radiated all the hospitality of a cage. Behind the wall surrounding the bungalow, two heavily armed policemen patrolled day and night, but that wasn't nearly safe enough; between the house's sleeping and living quarters there was a barred fence that was locked at night. On the evening we went out to dinner, I was only allowed to get out of the back seat once the restaurant guards had taken position on both sides of the car door; during the five metres of sidewalk we crossed, they hung over us as though we were visiting dignitaries; they walked along with us, matching our steps, holding their Sten guns at the ready. It all seemed a bit overdone to me, but I knew the statistics, and they encouraged you to the kind of caution that made you less than a shadow in a city in the throes of guerrilla warfare. In Carácas, between seventy and one hundred and twenty people were murdered each week; as soon as night fell, hordes of youthful criminals came down from the slums on the slopes and swarmed out across the neighbourhoods where the more affluent play; once those boys have reached the age of fourteen they are among the elders of their peer group, and have no qualms about emptying a full clip into a passer-by just to rob him of his tennis shoes.

Of the flamboyant Carácas that had embraced Truffino, little more remained than the hotel that had given him work; the Tamanaco is still a city within the city, although it has gradually come to resemble more a fortress amid the hills overrun with rickety huts. It was only during the embassy reception that I experienced something of the atmosphere of days gone by; most of the guests had come to the Country of Eternal Spring in the 1950s, and were nostalgic about the days back when they had traded in their bicycle for a station wagon, when all there was to worry about was what colour suit to wear to the next cocktail party – white, or a sophisticated grey. Back then, a litre of gasoline cost less than a litre of water.

At the end of my reading, I asked whether anyone had known Rudy Truffino; during the cold buffet on the embassy lawn, an elderly lady came up to me and said that Rudy had always stopped in to visit her when he was in Carácas. 'The last time he came, his brother was with him.' I asked her where that brother lived, and she vaguely recalled: 'Somewhere in the Gooi.'

Back in the Netherlands – many months later – I looked for him in the phone book. It turned out he lived in Naarden.

The house was spacious and solid, the way most town houses are that were built in the Gooi in the 1930s; it had a classical interior – Chesterfield sofa, flowery prints, lots of copper around the hearth, paintings on the walls. Ingrid served coffee in porcelain cups, presented sugar in a silver bowl and cream from a little silver pitcher; Han put a framed photo down on the coffee table, the portrait of Rudy made by the Swiss photographer Karl Weidmann, who had also taken the pictures I had seen hanging at Ucaima.

Han sat down across from that portrait and the resemblance was striking, he could have been Rudy's twin brother. And there was something else about him that resembled his brother as well: Rudy's voice, they way I'd heard it on tape, had been almost exactly like Han's. When I told him that, however, he waved away my comment.

'The differences are much more important. I'm chicken-hearted, but Rudy wasn't afraid of anything.'

He characterized his brother as an eccentric – then added 'like most Truffinos', with a grin that could have been prompted by either pride or chagrin.

'Strange people, my family; as Italian as the opera, but at the same time as "The Hague" as Eline Vere.'

The Dutch chapter of the family history began in the 19th century, when the goldsmith Carlo Giuseppe Domenico Truffino left his hometown of Pognana on Lake Como for Holland. The first king of the Netherlands had appointed him his court jeweller. It appears that Willem I also had an ulterior motive for bringing the Italian to Holland: Truffino was married to Marta Maria Peverelli, who combined in herself everything the king found desirable in a Mediterranean beauty. Not all of Maria's nine children, the rumour of the day had it, had been sired by the goldsmith. A hundred and fifty years later Rudy Truffino would joke to Prince Bernhard about having Orange blood in his veins.

Giuseppe and Marta Truffino arrived in the Netherlands around 1820. They crossed the Alps on foot; the only thing Giuseppe had with him was a spyglass, one of those retractable copper telescopes. When Rudy Truffino left Holland in 1951 to make a new life on the other side of the ocean, he – with a fine sense of tradition – took with him only that spyglass – I had found it in his library, amid his collection of pipes.

Willem I paid Giuseppe well; shortly after arrival he was able to buy a shop on what was then by far the most fashionable street in Amsterdam, the Rokin. 'Truffino Juweliers' was what the sign said, and under that, 'Purveyor to the Royal Household'. The shop remained in existence for three generations.

The fourth generation Truffino moved to The Hague, and used the family capital made in jewellery to start a banking house. Truffino & Co. set up business on the Veenkade in 1890. By then the family was fully assimilated, the bank was run by Henricus and Willem Truffino; the third brother, Lodewijk, became general manager of the Dutch postal service. Their way of life, however, always kept a certain southern element. Each week, Willem had himself driven in his coach to the Association of Arts and Sciences, and before he had ordered his first drink his eye would be drawn to the tightly corseted waists of the demimondaines. After countless amorous escapades, he was forced to flee abroad – he went to Paris. His son Henricus – Rudy and Han's father – took over the bank in 1918 at the age of twenty-one, along with his brother Willem.

Truffino & Co. was a distinctly Catholic financial institution. Taking advantage of his Italian surname, Rudy's grandfather had succeeded in extending a great many loans to churches, monastic orders and other religious organizations in Germany, usually in the form of bond issues. The Dutch clientele was of a more private nature, but no less Catholic. With eight or nine employees, Truffino & Co. remained a small bank, which didn't bother Rudy's father much; even in the lean thirties his bank turned a healthy profit, until the political climate changed in Germany and the money loaned to his Eastern clients was frozen in the form of *Sperrmarken*.

The Truffino house had warm water from the tap, the stoves

purred and there were steaming pans of food on the table each evening, but the atmosphere was no less chilly for all that. The children were allowed to take turns once a week eating at the table with their parents, on condition that they remained silent unless spoken to. On all other days they ate in the playroom, under the watchful eye of the maid and the nanny.

Mother Truffino came from a family that was every bit as wealthy as her husband's – she was the youngest daughter of the Van der Lugts, the insurance family from Rotterdam – and every bit as Catholic; she had been educated by the nuns, in French, at a convent school. Han described her as strict, distant and completely without feeling. It was only at the table that she established sporadic contact with her children; the actual upbringing she left to the governess, while the youngest children were bathed and clothed by the housekeeper.

Louis was the oldest of the five; his family nickname was 'Ipy'. Annie soon came to be seen as the most intelligent, she later went to Leiden to study law, then eloped with a Swiss man just before her finals and moved to the Alps. At home, Annie was called 'Tutty', her younger sister Giovanna had to make do with 'Poppy'. Then came Han – 'Broer' to his family – followed on December 7th, 1928 by Rudolf, the youngest, who his mother called 'Janus Tea-leaf' – she considered him a fabulist, and as soon as he entered the dining room she would say: 'I'm warning you, button your lip.'

To make use of their *Sperrmarken*, which had lost three-quarters of their rate of exchange abroad and could be spent at face value only inside Germany itself, the family always went east for the summer holidays; every winter as well, father, mother, the five children, the governess and the maid would spend a few weeks at the ski resorts of Bavaria or Sauerland. The children's shoes and clothes were bought in

Germany; their book bags, coloured pencils, toy trains, dolls and tinker toys were also acquired during the holidays. Due to their frequent stays at health and ski resorts, the children spoke a polished and stately kind of German, and felt as much at home in Germany as they did in The Hague.

Han told me about the four weeks in summer the family had spent in the Eifel, the holiday in the winter of 1937-1938 at Winterberg in Sauerland, the summer vacation in 1938 at Titisee in the Black Forest, the winter vacation in 1938-1939 at Hotel Sonnebichel in Garmisch Partenkirchen, the summer of 1939 at Werninge Roode, close to the Harz Mountains, and the cruise which the family made later that same year on a German ship from Bremen to the Canary Islands. In September of that year the war started, the ship remained anchored off Vigo, and it took the family weeks to return overland to the Netherlands. Despite the unfortunate end to their holiday, however, the children didn't fully realize what was going on around them. 'How many Dutch people ever went skiing in those days? How many Dutch people spent their holidays on a cruise ship? We lived,' Han recalled from the vantage of adulthood, 'in a dream, and the only thing that interested us was whether the home movies Father made during our vacations turned out well.' After the war, he was sometimes haunted by very different images, things that had also caught his childish eyes in those days: Hitler, in the streets of Titisee, arm uplifted at the head of a delirious procession; or the young boys in Kreefeld, the day they had popped across the border with their mother to buy clothes, who had first clicked their heels obsequiously and then, a moment later, wanted to fight with them because they refused to buy their *Hitlerjugend* paper. But back when they were still in knee pants, Germany had mostly meant luxury, and new clothes, and presents.

The family spent the shorter holidays, at Easter or Whitsuntide or in the fall, in the woods of the Dutch Veluwe, where Mrs. Truffino had had a holiday home built with the money from an inheritance. In the Veluwe, too, the big bad world seemed infinitely far away as the children built their treehuts in the woods.

The outbreak of war didn't immediately put an end to the period of prosperity and easy living; on the contrary, after the German invasion the *Sperrmarken* were suddenly worth as much as they were in Germany itself, and at one fell swoop Father Truffino was free of all financial cares. But as from the second year of the war, the family barely profited from that anymore.

Although he regarded banking as an amusing game which he could play with conviction if need be, Henricus Truffino saw himself more as an artist. He painted, and at the end of every afternoon he changed from his three-piece suit into an old smock and locked himself up in his atelier, or hurried off to the Pulchri Studio, where he surrounded himself with actors and artists. They were drawn to the bottles of wine which he upturned so freely, he was content with their anecdotes, which made him feel that he belonged with people of a different ilk, people who lived more intensely and sought more fervently for the unattainable. He spent most of his free hours associating with painters, and took lessons twice a week from the famous Hague painter Jos Croin. A few of his father's paintings still hung on the wall at Han's house: ominous skies, puny farms, subdued landscapes that pay homage with every brushstroke to the masters of The Hague School.

Croin lived with a much younger woman, whom Truffino saw as his ideal model. He convinced her to pose for him, fell passionately in love with her, bought an apartment so he could see her every day. He was no man to cut corners, and soon he bought a gorgeous residence on Noordeinde and had it put in her name. But he was unable to keep his liaison a secret for long. When his wife found out, she threw him out of the house. The divorce became final in the winter of 1941 -1942.

In staunch Catholic circles, the Truffinos had commited the unforgivable. Han and Rudy's playmates stopped talking to them. Even the older children no longer dared to go to church, because the entire congregation looked the other way when they kneeled at the altar. An air of frivolity had always surrounded the family, and the leading residents of The Hague now saw their suspicions confirmed: the grandfather had run away to Paris, and the father had ruined his reputation for the sake of a tramp.

Once Father Truffino was divorced, he stopped caring what people thought of him: he had always despised the bourgeois life at bottom, and with all the élan of the late-bloomer he rushed headlong into one affair after the other. The woman he had considered his muse deserted him; once she'd settled into the house on Noordeinde, Truffino was no longer allowed to come by. To his wife's fury, he and his next girlfriend moved into the holiday home on the Veluwe; other demanding and expensive affairs followed, until, at the end of the war, he married Hans, with whom he spent the rest of his life. Seven years after the war was over, he was financially ruined; with his own hands, he built a house on a plot of pastureland he had bought for a pittance close to the lakes at Nieuwkoop; then he built a dyke around a pool, pumped it dry and built a second house, which he then sold. It made him just enough money to keep him from starving in his old age, although whenever one of the children came to visit he would warn them beforehand: 'Be sure to bring something to eat with you.' Halfway through the 1950s he was forced to sell the bank, but that didn't make him much money either; most of what he transferred to the new owner were debts.

Of Rudy and his father, Han said: 'A pair of scamps if I ever saw one.' They went hunting together in the polder, skinned the hares they'd shot and prepared gargantuan meals together. Father let him taste the wine, Father didn't object when he took a puff of his cigar, Father laughed loudest at his jokes. But Rudy didn't see his father often.

The children remained living with their mother, in the big townhouse on Albertinestraat in the Bezuidenhout neighbourhood, an area so bourgeois and so quintessentially of The Hague that Louis Couperus had chosen it as the place where Eline Vere, the Dutch Emma Bovary, put an end to her life: it was on Bezuidenhoutseweg that she hung herself from a lamppost. The oldest houses in the neighbourhood dated from the fin de siècle, the most modern from the belle époque, and by the end of the 1930s they had all started looking alike in their dilapidation.

After the divorce, Mother Truffino could no longer afford a maid or a governess. Suddenly she had to take care of her children herself, and she had five mouths to feed. Groceries were rationed by that time, and the longer the war lasted, the greater the sacrifice that had to be made for every coupon. Han said it was 'by a miracle' that they were able to get enough food, even during the final, harsh winter of 1944-1945.

Two months before the end of the war, however, the family lost everything that had not already been sold, hocked or frittered away. On Saturday, March 3rd, 1945, due to an error on the part of the RAF's Second Tactical Unit, English pilots dropped seven hundred bombs on Bezuidenhout. The entire

Rudy Truffino as an extra in *Green Mansions*
(photo: R. Truffino archives)

A publicity shot of stars Audrey Hepburn and Anthony Perkins
in *Green Mansions*

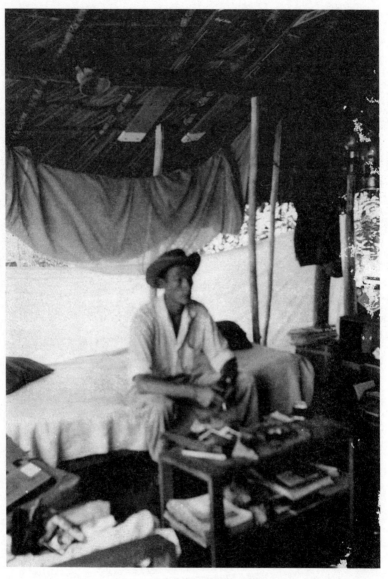

Rudy Truffino in the first camp he built, at Canaima
(photo: R. Truffino archives)

Ucaima in 1988, during the rainy season
(photo: H. Truffino archives)

Jimmy Angel
(photo from Ruth Robertson's *Churún Méru - The Tallest Angel*)

The 1963 orchid expedition to the top of the Auyán Tepui. In front
the bearers, followed by Rudy Truffino (photo: R. Truffino archives)

Truffino with Canadian Prime Minister Trudeau, 1978
(photo: *Canada Weekly*)

The five Truffino children on a skiing holiday. Left to right: Poppy,
Han, Ipy, Tuty, Rudy (photo: H. Truffino archives)

Rudy Truffino in Germany, 1939 (photo: H. Truffino archives)

Rudy Truffino on the savanna west of Ucaima
(photo: H. Truffino)

The mountains with the petroglyphs: the Venado Tepui
(photo: O. Hendriksz)

Angel Falls
(photo: R. Truffino)

Rudy Truffino on the Auyán Tepui during the first orchid
expedition in 1963 (photo: R. Truffino archives)

Gaby in the hammock with her Pemón playmates
(photo: R. Truffino)

The Yanomami
(photo: R. Truffino)

Gerti and Rudy Truffino, 1962 (photo: R. Truffino archives)

Rudy with his daughter Lily, close to Angel Falls, 1978
(photo: R. Truffino archives)

Han and Rudy on the way to Angel Falls
(photo: H. Truffino archives)

The 1963 orchid expedition. To Truffino's right, Francisco Monte de Oca. To the far right, Nora and Galfrid Dunsterville (photo: R. Truffino archive)

neighbourhood was destroyed; only half a wall of the Truffinos' house on Albertinestraat remained standing, with the staircase dangling in thin air.

The bombardment did not come as a complete surprise. Bombs, intended for the fortifications at Benoordenhout and the greenbelt at Bezuidenhout, where V-2 rockets were launched against England, had fallen on the neighbourhood earlier that same week as well. Many of the neighbours had already left on Thursday and Friday, after a number of explosions had blown deep craters in eight streets and destroyed several houses. On Friday afternoon, the house next door took a direct hit: the explosion was so powerful that all the window in the Truffino's house were blown out, the front door flew into the street, the back door knocked a whole in the kitchen wall, and the ceilings buckled. By that time Han and Ipy were no longer living on Albertinestraat; a few months earlier they had gone into hiding in the attic of their father's bank on the Veenkade, to avoid the press gangs – the house on Albertinestraat was directly across from the police station, and according to Han all the policemen there were Nazi sympathizers. After the bomb hit next door, Rudy borrowed a cart from the local baker and filled it with things which were, in Han's eyes, completely useless: a bookshelf, a toy train, a photo of the five children on skis: odds and ends. He pushed the cart to the Veenkade, where he spent the night. Mrs. Truffino and the two girls remained in the house on Albertinestraat. That same evening they buried a few heirlooms; when they came back two weeks later, the only things that had survived among the charred remains were the oil-and-vinegar set, the copper coal scuttle and the copper pans.

The next morning Han and Rudy looked out the window of the top floor on the Veenkade and saw sixteen or eighteen bombers appear above The Hague. The planes disappeared into a cloud, and from that cloud it then began raining bombs. A series of explosions followed less than a minute later. Because of the haze that covered the city, they couldn't tell exactly where the bombs had fallen – at first they thought it had been a way south of the Bezuidenhout neighbourhood. What they could see was that the Bethlehem Clinic had been hit, and was burning. Until mid-morning, Rudy and Ipy shuttled the baker's cart back and forth between the maternity clinic and a hastily set-up field hospital, carrying women who had just given birth or were just going into labour. At the field hospital a doctor told them that Bezuidenhout had been hit particularly hard. They fetched Han and went immediately to Albertinestraat, but the sea of flames they met along the way melted the soles of their shoes, and they were unable to reach their home. The crowds of people fleeing in the other direction also blocked their way; after the planes dropped their payloads, they had swung full circle and strafed the neighbourhood with machine-gun fire; the bullets whistled through the wreckage and the crowd rushed ahead in mortal fear, hitting and kicking anything that got in their way. The only thing Rudy ever tried to put into words later, when his daughters asked about growing up in Holland, was that moment when everyone lost their minds. 'My pot-bellied stove, my pot-bellied stove,' he would moan, imitating a gurgling sob; while the whole neighbourhood was on fire and the heat singed the hair off your head, he had seen an old man sitting on his ruined doorstep, sobbing because he had been unable to save his pot-bellied stove from the inferno.

'More salvos,' an eyewitness reported years later – his

account was included in the memorial volume published by the Dutch 'March 3' Foundation – '…and again, and again. The ground heaved; we heard screams, moans. It kept getting darker. Then we saw the fire. The people in the street started panicking. People came running out of their houses, carrying children in their arms or pulling a crib behind them. People were trampled underfoot. Others collapsed in fear, and then came the bombers again, firing their machine-guns into the fleeing crowd. We passed the Schenkkade. The Catholic church there had been badly damaged. The steeple was split in two, the presbytery was only a smoking ruin. Entire rows of houses flattened. We kept running. Behind us bombs, bombs, bombs, fire, screaming, clouds of dust, maddening fear everywhere. Terrible, unbearable. Three squadrons of eighteen bombers each were responsible for this slaughter. The attack was so off-target that our Bezuidenhout neighbourhood was completely destroyed, while the V2s could be launched routinely that same day. Hundreds and hundreds of people were killed, the number of wounded must have been beyond count.'

The next day Han, Ipy and Rudy tried to get into the neighbourhood again, but by then it had been cordoned off tightly by the army and the police. The initial list of victims was published around noon; their mother and sisters were not on it, but many of their neighbours were. They returned to the Veenkade, not speaking a word; they thought nothing, did nothing, and had no idea what to say. The next day brought no news, nor did the day after. Only five or six days later did they finally hear that their mother and sisters had fled to the town of Voorburg, and were relatively unharmed.

'Run!' their mother had shouted when the first bombs hit the street. One of the girls wanted to take a fur coat with her, she ran to her room but, halfway up the stairs, she turned back; the roof had already been blown off the house. They ran down the street, stumbling over dead bodies. From Albertinestraat they went to the nearby soccer stadium; the carnage there was even worse, bodies without arms, legs, heads, so they ran on to the railroad viaduct. In all the confusion they became separated and found each other again only the next day, in Voorburg. Friends of the family gave them a place to sleep, and that is where Han, Ipy and Rudy finally located them, 'three desperate creatures, in a village with thousands of desperate people walking around, not yet fully aware of what had happened to them.'

The bombardment of Bezuidenhout took the lives of five hundred and twenty people, wounded an unknown number, and left twelve thousand people homeless. The mistake was caused by the sudden cloud cover, and by an error on the part of a British officer; he had mistakenly switched around level and plumb. To calculate the precise target – the place where the V2s were launched – he drew the horizontal line at 064 (should have been 042) and the vertical line 042 (should have been 064). The two lines intersected in the heart of the Bezuidenhout neighbourhood, twelve hundred metres from the actual target. The exact point where the lines crossed was the street where Rudy Truffino had grown up.

After the war, the children remained at the Veenkade for a while. 'Come stay with us,' they told their mother, but Ma had no intention whatsoever of moving in with her ex-husband. She stayed with friends, an aunt, an uncle, until she was finally allocated a house on Van Montfortlaan in the Benoordenhout neighbourhood. The children were reunited with her there in December of 1945, but Rudy had barely hung the bookshelf back on the wall to hold his pride and joy – the short-wave radio with which he could receive stations from all over the hemisphere – before he was itching to leave again.

Han didn't have the slightest idea which school his youngest brother had attended, or whether he had even seen the inside of a classroom at all during the war. 'He was always off messing around,' was all Han could remember; Rudy fought with his mother all the time, and would run out of the house and not come back for days. And when he did come back at last, the fights resumed and reached such a pitch that Rudy sometimes hit his mother. That was why Han could never understand why Rudy, once in Venezuela, had added his mother's maiden name to his, and why 'Truffino van der Lugt' was written on his grave. He categorically dismissed the idea that it could be seen as a belated apology; according to Han, Rudy held a grudge against his mother all his life. 'Truffino van der Lugt' just sounded snootier than 'Truffino', Han figured that had to be it. And in Venezuela, with its hundreds of thousands of immigrants from Sicily, Naples and Bari, it sounded less Italian, and therefore less shabby. Because that was one point about which Han was quite resolute: Rudy had never been able to accept the fact that the Truffinos had fallen on hard times, and that the grandeur in which the family had lived before the war had been lost. He blamed almost everyone for that loss, except the man whose fault it was: his father.

As a boy, Rudy had been small, skinny, fragile. At the age of sixteen he still looked like a twelve year old; those who didn't know him treated him as a child, even though the war made boys his age grow up quickly. He tried to seem older as well, by smoking (when he could get hold of cigarettes, that is: tobacco was scarce as well), by ignoring all attempts to tell him what to do, by shooting his mouth off. None of which made him any more imposing, of course; he remained a pipsqueak.

During the second or third year of the war, Rudy was expelled from high school. He entered art academy, but when his father asked the director of the academy a few months later how his son was getting along, it turned out he had never attended a class.

And after that? Han couldn't remember. He'd had as little idea of how to deal with Rudy as his mother had; the only person Rudy was close to was Ipy, the oldest boy. When I suggested that Ipy might be able to tell me more about that period, Han shook his head – since Ipy's brain haemorrhage, he didn't remember much anymore. And their sister Tutty? When she was pregnant with her sixth child, Tutty had fallen down the stairs and broken her neck. And Poppy, the oldest girl? Poppy had died in 1982.

Rudy had no more desire to go to school, that much was clear. He hung around at the hockey rink, wandered through town. A month after the liberation he filched his father's car keys, picked up three of his friends and raced off to Amsterdam. He was seventeen. After spending two nights in the jazz cafés on Leidseplein, he showed up in The Hague again, walked into his father's office, laid the car keys on the desk and said: 'Thanks, Pop, it was a lot of fun.'

After the war, all three of the Truffino boys went to work at their father's bank. Rudy spent months just twiddling his thumbs. To him, the only interesting thing about money was being able to spend it yourself; that other people gave their money to his father for safekeeping only demonstrated to him that they were too wishy-washy to enjoy life. He wanted to see the world, he wanted to do crazy things. One evening, when Ipy was locking up the bank's safe, he noticed that the gun they always kept lying there had disappeared. He was in favour of warning the police right away, but Han thought he knew who might be behind it: Rudy. They went to his room and found him fast asleep, the gun under his pillow.

During banking hours he would sit and stare out the window, or pore over the atlas. 'I'm not a man to be stuck inside,' he told his father, after months of doing nothing. So Father Truffino sent him to work in the Noordoost Polder, which had just been drained. Rudy spent two years digging ditches, milking cows and helping farmers birth their calves. There was plenty of space in the new polder, but it still wasn't exactly what he'd expected from life. Later, when Venezuelans or Americans would ask him what Holland was like, he would tell them: 'The rain falls three hundred days a year on soaking-wet ground that's flat as a pancake, and no tree in sight for as far as you can see.'

It was his Swiss brother-in-law who finally freed him from the mud. There was nothing particularly eccentric about his oldest sister's husband, the owner of a porcelain factory, yet he surrounded himself with dreamers of various ilk. One of those friends had purchased a huge tract of desert in Tunisia; he planned to turn the area southwest of Grombalia into a grazing belt, and he was desperately in need of hard-working young fellows. Holland was too cramped for Rudy, he was ready to leave; he signed a contract for six months, then left for Marseille on a wing and a prayer. In Tunisia he earned almost nothing, he barely received anything to eat, he was treated like a coolie and had to sleep in a bunk in a scorching-hot barrack amid twenty or thirty other hastily drummed-up farm workers. He came down with malaria, and the next recurrence left him stumbling to the latrine with severe stomach cramps.

About six months after he had left Holland, the Dutch consul in Tunis sent a telegram to his father to say that 'a

certain Rudy Truffino, possibly your son' was lying in a run-
down pension in that city, at death's door. Father Truffino left
immediately for Tunis, but Rudy refused to go home with
him. To demonstrate to his father that there was nothing for
him to worry about, he got up, put on a suit, and showed him
around Tunis. His father returned to The Hague, not
suspecting that it was morphine that had kept his son on his
feet that whole day. Only weeks later, when malaria felled him
again and he could see no other way out, did Rudy accept the
fact that he hadn't succeeded on his own, and asked the Dutch
consul for money for the trip home.

Han met him at the station in The Hague.

When Rudy got down off the train, he was puffing on a
big Havana.

'Where did you get that?' asked Hans, who had expected to
see his brother come stumbling up to him, more dead than alive.

'Oh, I was sitting across from this priest and he was
smoking these big, fat cigars, one after the other. At a certain
point I said to him: "Christ Almighty, man, either put that
thing out or give me one..." So he gave me two of them.'

The first thing Han saw of the Dutch East Indies was the mouth of the Musi. The troop-ship dropped anchor offshore; a sloop took him ashore, and after four weeks he was finally feeling solid ground beneath his feet again. Conscripted into military service and then shipped off right away to South-Sumatra – it wasn't what he'd been hoping for, so soon after the war. Before he'd even learned how to really handle a rifle, he found himself in a gun battle with the nationalist rebels; during the seven months that followed, there wasn't a moment when he didn't fear for his life. Then an eye disease relieved him of any further duties in the police action; after being treated at the military hospital in Batavia, he was given a medical discharge. He returned to the Netherlands, half-blind. But once at home, he found himself regularly shutting his eyes to summon up the sunsets that had flamed so hotly they had turned the sky, the trees and the earth a fiery red. He recommended that his youngest brother seek his fortune in Asia, but Rudy wasn't interested – wasn't Asia crawling with people? Even back then Rudy knew he wanted to go into the jungle, as far from the crowds as possible.

What Rudy had actually been up to while he was in the East Indies, Han couldn't remember; maybe he really had taken a course in veterinary medicine. In any event, among the things he packed when he went to the Dominican

Republic were a dozen hypodermic needles. He left in May of 1951; that he was entering the employ of General Rafael Leonidas Trujillo, one of South America's most loathsome dictators, a man who had held his country in a torturous grip for more than two decades, didn't seem to bother him. And Trujillo was a genocidal murderer to boot: he'd had ten to twenty thousand Haitians killed, to cleanse his country of black influence. A man who had appropriated six hundred thousand hectares of farmland to build a personal fortune which, when he was killed in 1961, was estimated at five hundred million dollars.

'I don't think Rudy knew any of that,' Han supposed. He just needed to find a job somewhere, and when he saw that ad in *The Times* he figured he was cut out for it. That naiveté — or was it shortsightedness? — had almost cost him his life.

He had once told Han: 'I got along wonderfully with his children, and I learned horseback riding on the *haciendas*. I had a splendid time, but I almost pissed myself on the way to the firing squad. I shouted at them that they hadn't heard the last of this yet, that Holland would send a brace of military vessels over from Curaçao if they harmed even a hair on my head. They laughed themselves silly.'

By late 1952, he was wandering around Carácas like a tramp. Rudy later made it all sound more exotic than it was; in fact, he had simply lived in the gutter. Han said the story about a manager of the Tamanaco Hotel being charmed by Rudy's foreign accent was just a myth. But his German was indeed impeccable, in Tunisia he had learned to speak a good bit of French, in the Dominican Republic his Spanish had advanced by leaps and bounds, and he had listened to the BBC all through the war.

He barely stayed in contact with his family after he left; during the forty-four years he spent on the other side of the ocean, he sent no more than ten letters to the Netherlands, and that was including birth announcements and changes of address. He considered it unlikely that he would ever see his family again; the boat trip to Venezuela took about four weeks, and the plane was too expensive for a private person. His parents, brothers and sisters heard only years later that he had moved to Canaima, and much later still that he had gotten married. The family sent a telegram to congratulate him. I found it amid the wedding photos; it was posted on January 14th to Cíudad Bolívar, and arrived in Canaima on January 23rd. Rudy was, indeed, gone from the world.

The flights with Charlie Baughan, his months with the Indians, the first camp at Canaima, the second one at Ucaima

– the family heard about all this only in the late 1960s, when contact was reestablished. His father decided to visit him in Venezuela. He didn't have the money for a plane, but for a modest sum he could ship aboard a Shell tanker that was leaving Rotterdam for Maracaibo. He was just about to leave when his youngest daughter gave her mother a trip to Ucaima, for her sixty-fifth birthday. The prospect of sitting in a canoe with his ex-wife ruined old Truffino's fun before he'd even left, so he stayed home. And so Rudy flew from Carácas to Canaima, not with his father, but with his mother; he was so infuriated that, before putting the plane down in the Gran Sabana, he first flew through the canyons around the *tepuis*, almost touching the wing to the rock walls. His mother took the opportunity to ask whether he had actually earned his pilot's license. He edged the plane up a little closer to the wall and said: 'No, Ma, here you don't earn your license, you buy it.' He installed his mother at Canaima, regretted that soon enough, and the next day took her upstream to his camp. His father died one year later; the next in the long line of things for which Rudy blamed his mother was that her pushiness had spoiled his last chance to see his father. But he did hang up a picture of her, in his office.

Ipy came to visit the Gran Sabana in the early 1970s; he stayed for about six weeks. After that, Rudy lost contact with his family again.

One afternoon in the autumn of 1979, the doorbell rang at the Truffino house in Naarden. Han wasn't home, his wife Ingrid opened the door. The first thing she saw was a taxi in the drive, the second a man in khaki wandering around the front yard. She had never met him, but she said: 'You must be Rudy.'

He grinned.

'The black sheep of the family. That's right.'

Han knew Rudy well enough, he knew he hadn't simply come by for a visit. He had become a Venezuelan citizen, and he had told Ipy eight years earlier that he never planned to go back to Holland again.

After a few days, Rudy began talking about his financial situation. He was making enough money now, but it seems he'd made a complete mess of the bookkeeping.

'All those numbers get on my nerves.'

Ipy had already offered to impose a little order on his bookkeeping, and Han provided him with advice as well. Han had an engineering firm in Naarden; Ipy had remained with his father's bank till the bitter end, and had then moved to another banking house. Both of them knew how to manage money, both were able to invest the little bit Rudy had left at the end of each year in a way that would yield some income once he was no longer able to work. Because both brothers had come to the same realization: Rudy was already past fifty, and had started wondering what he was going to live on once he could no longer climb mountains or wrestle boats through rapids.

But other things had brought him to Holland as well. He had taken Neil Armstrong to Angel Falls, and Canadian prime minister Trudeau, who like it so much that he had returned within the year; he had received Princess Margaret, Prince Charles, Prince Bernhard, and to keep the family from failing to notice what a legend he had become, he had decided to come and tell them about it himself.

'Special people,' he expounded to his brother, 'are special in everything they do, the same way assholes never learn not to be assholes about even the most minor details.' He appreciated how all these famous people were willing to put up with cold showers at Ucaima and the hardships they encountered on their trips through the interior. It was also clear to him why

141

the VIPs preferred the backwoods to the Waldorf Astoria; in the jungle you might step on a coral snake or a rattlesnake, but there weren't any paparazzi lurking in the bushes. At Ucaima they could do as they liked, which was not to say they abandoned their quirks.

A few weeks before Prince Bernhard arrived, Truffino had received from the Dutch embassy a long list of everything His Royal Highness liked to smoke, drink and eat, and what he definitely could not stand. According to the list, the prince couldn't stand chicken. Truffino had hare flown in specially from Carácas for the prince, and *cordero*, a type of Australian mutton; for the other guests he simply put a few drumsticks on the barbecue. During the first meal, a buffet beneath the big tree by the river, Bernhard went immediately for the chicken. But before he could sink his teeth into the drumstick, Rudy shouted: 'Wait a minute, Bernhard, what is this? You don't eat chicken!' To which the prince replied, with a sigh, that it had been years since he'd had a nice drumstick. 'Well no wonder, the list says you can't stand chicken.' The prince thought about it, then recalled that once, long ago, he had become ill after a meal of chicken.

The list also said that the prince enjoyed a little armagnac after his meal. To get hold of armagnac on the South American continent was, in Truffino's words, 'Jesus-fucking-impossible'. After a great many phone calls, he found out that there was an American hotel on the island of Margarita with a few bottles in its cellar. Rudy bought a ticket and asked a lady friend to fly to Margarita and come back with at least six bottles. The armagnac arrived in Ucaima just in time. But all the fuss was for nothing: the prince was also perfectly content with the Argentine wine Truffino had bought. After the first glass, he asked: 'How much of this wine do you have?' 'Two cases.' 'Okay, give the others whisky and beer, you and I are going to finish that wine, it tastes fine to me.'

Finally, the list said, after dinner the prince enjoyed smoking a good cigar of the brand H. Uppmann. The cigars were like the bottles of armagnac: they had to be brought in from Margarita, and years later there were still two boxes of them, unopened, under the bar.

'But okay,' Truffino grinned when Millicent Smeets interviewed him in 1984, 'at least I was knighted for it.' A few months after the prince's visit, the embassy let him know that he had been appointed Knight in the Order of Oranje Nassau. He pinned the decoration to the lining in the lid of his suitcase; whenever he had to open it at the border, they always let him through right away.

There was one thing Rudy didn't tell his brothers, and he never said at thing to Millicent about it either. Han discovered it by accident, while trying to arrange Rudy's finances.

The prince and his retinue had spent five days at Ucaima. After they left, Truffino sent an invoice to the Dutch embassy in Carácas. When the sum still hadn't been transferred to his account weeks later, Truffino contacted them to ask whether the invoice had arrived. But even after the second reminder, the bill still wasn't paid. For the visit by His Royal Highness, the adjutant, the private secretary, the two ambassadors and both co-pilots, Rudy never received a cent.

Charles was even more presumptuous; he assumed that Truffino would be honoured to have the Prince of Wales stay at his camp, and never said a word about payment.

Princess Margaret was a bit more courteous; after she left, she had two outboard motors delivered to Ucaima, in thanks for the care taken. Unfortunately, the motors proved too heavy for a *curiare*, and years later they were still hanging in the boathouse, rusting away.

After all those blue-blooded visits, Truffino was in deep financial trouble. *Emmanuelle VI* was one way out. On the day the film crew left, the producer paid his bill on the spot and handed the Indians who had steered the boats an envelope with cash; a gesture Rudy greatly appreciated.

In 1980, Han and Ingrid went to Venezuela. Every evening they sat around the table in the open hut Rudy had built beside the river and listened to his stories.

Gerti didn't mingle with the others. She understood no Dutch, and whenever Han and Ingrid switched to German Gerti would speak three sentences and disappear into the kitchen. Gerti was always busy, maniacally busy, in the kitchen, in the office or the shed, where she did the ironing.

At the dinner table they tried it again, this time in German. Rudy told them about the first years at Ucaima, and Gerti interrupted him only once. 'Everything he says is totally true.'

They took the dugout up to Angel Falls; for once, Gerti let them talk her into going along. But almost as soon as they got to the lodge, she brought the children to bed, then turned in herself.

'I got suckered into it,' Rudy said a few glasses of wine later, staring into the glowing hearth.

Han didn't quite understand.

'She got pregnant.'

When he met her, he had found her pretty, agile, brave, modern, but he had absolutely no intention of starting a family in the jungle. But she wouldn't leave him alone, every time he flew to Canaima, she had to go with him. Maybe she had loved Canaima even more than he did; one look at the waterfalls was enough to make her rapturous. And listen, he wasn't a block of stone either; when she went scrambling over the rocks he couldn't keep his eyes off those long, muscular legs. And whenever she'd button up her aviator suit after a dip in the river, he found her completely irresistible. She had something else he liked, something only Han could understand; her manners reminded him of the old family holidays, of the guests at the health resorts and the women in line for the lift at Garmisch Partenkirchen. She may have been drawn to wild and rugged country, but the language she spoke was every bit as polished as the German he had heard in the hotels as a child. Their forefathers had even had the same profession; Giuseppe Truffino had made Willem I's crown, Gerti's grandfather had forged the ring for the bishop of Salzburg. They were both from a Europe that barely existed anymore, and that was important when you were miles away from anywhere, where only the books they brought along had anything to do with that civilization. They shared a love of nature as well; there was nothing he enjoyed more than looking at plants and flowers with her. And, well, she admired him endlessly, and that left him defenceless. When she'd told him she was already two months pregnant, he had seen it as his duty to marry her.

The first few years they'd had a clear, common goal. They were of the same mind, had been poor together, went through hard times. He had never really been in love with her, but he gained respect for Gerti, who never used her womanhood as an excuse when the time came to drag and carry, chop and build. He found it moving to see her at the cement mixer in the early morning light, it touched him at the end of the day when she put her hands behind her back to hide the blood and the scrapes. After every setback he could find the words to buck her up, and she would go right back to work. In between times, the children took all their attention; at first it was just fun to see them running around naked in the jungle, but later they had to learn reading, writing and arithmetic, and that took a lot of energy. In fact, he had never really liked the idea of having children in the jungle, he often asked himself what he' d gotten into; he was afraid they would blame him later on for making them miss a good education. After the first few years at home and at the Indian school in Canaima, he sent them to the Von Humboldt boarding school in Carácas. Then the girls only came back to Ucaima for the holidays, and the rest of the time he was stuck there with Gerti.

He felt like a fish in the water when he had an audience; Gerti was as tight as a clam. And so Rudi used to busy himself with the guests while she worked in the kitchen, served the meals, did the washing and cleaned the rooms. He thought all that work was a waste of her energy. After all, they could just hire a few Indians to do that. But hiring people cost money, and Gerti was terrified that they would have to go hungry again, the way they had at first.

During the rainy season, when there were sometimes no guests for months on end, they were completely at each other's mercy. It never took long for the fighting to start. Whenever she disagreed with him, he read that as contempt, or as ridicule at the very least. It finally got to the point where they lived apart in the same camp. He moved into the house on the far right side, she took the rooms in the oldest of the guesthouses, close to the river, on the extreme left. After the dishes were done, she started writing increasingly long letters to her old friends in Salzburg; after a final walk around the camp, he would go to the library and find himself a book to take to bed. When they saw each other again at breakfast they would nod grumpily, knowing full well that they depended on each other in order to keep the camp running. It irritated him that she was so cold, like his mother; it irritated her that he was always putting on a show for the guests and telling tall tales to draw the ladies' attention, while she had to make the beds and iron the sheets. He barely spoke to her anymore, and the only thing that still made her happy were the plants she'd planted all over the camp, and the orchids on the trees.

Later, among Gerti's correspondence, I found a letter that confirmed Rudy's confession to his brother and sister-in-law. It was a letter from 1978, written to Edith Vavken, who lived in Puerto Ordaz. Edith, born and raised in Berlin, became Gerti's sole confidante in Venezuela; she came to Ucaima three or four times a year, usually during the school holidays, and lightened Gerti's task by taking care of the children. Aunt Edith was soon a part of the family. It was also Edith Vavken who had once saved Rudy's life; she arrived at Canaima, and sat behind Rudy in the *curiare* on the way to Ucaima. As she was climbing out of the boat, she pointed to his ear and said to him: 'Man, you'd better start taking antibiotics right away. You've got leishmaniasis.' Edith was a molecular biologist.

Gerti had told Edith that she was thinking about divorcing Rudy. In her reply, Edith counseled her to give it some very good thought; after all, she had put years of work into the camp, and if she left now that would all be lost. And then there were the children; they had become completely Venezuelan, and they would surely want to stay in the country with Rudy. If she went back to Salzburg – which she was apparently considering – she would lose her daughters. Edith could imagine that it was 'almost impossible' for her to stay at the camp – the arguments with Rudy must have been fierce. But in the end, she said, Gerti had little choice; she could either abandon everything that was dear to her, or live with the situation, painful as that might be.

Gerti came to the same conclusion, and stayed.

Once the two oldest girls had finished secondary school, they returned to Ucaima. Lily, to her father's complete satisfaction, married a Venezuelan helicopter pilot. Rudy got along well with Raúl, who worked for the Venezuelan power company and made daily flights to see how much water was flowing off the Gran Sabana into the reservoir behind Guri Dam. Raúl Serrano also accompanied the reporters from *Geo* magazine when they came to the Gran Sabana; he spent weeks flying a geologist, a biologist and a photographer to the caves and crannies in the mesas. By way of grand finale, he steered his chopper through the Valley of the Thousand Pillars atop the Auyán Tepui, zigzagging between pillars of rock higher than the skyscrapers of Manhattan. On his way to yet another mesa, Raúl would often sing 'La Donna è Mobile' from *Rigoletto*. Raúl was a younger version of Rudy, in love with the area, in love with flying and discovery.

Lily went along with her father on most of his trips. She knew the Auyán Tepui as well as he did. There had to be a real specialist in the group for her to find out anything new about the reptiles, the carnivorous plants or the butterflies. She had learned it all without effort, from her parents, from the biologists and botanists onto whose laps she had climbed as a child, and from the Indian friends with whom she'd shared a hammock as a toddler. When Raúl came into the picture, Rudy felt that the future was secure; Lily would take over the camp from him, and Raúl would fly new groups of researchers to the mesas.

It was Gaby he was worried about.

One evening, during the time Han and Ingrid were visiting the camp, Gaby found an excuse to go to Canaima and only came back the next morning. Rudy was furious. He knew where she'd been: with those good-for-nothing Jiménez people, an antisocial family that had settled down by the tourist resort on the lagoon. They were half-Indian, half-Venezuelan. One of the Jiménez boys – the family had twelve children in total – was after Gaby. Juan was less than one metre fifty tall, and already bloated by beer despite his youth. It was a tossup whether he could read or write. Rudy called him the 'wood gnome', and when he heard that this dwarf was going to be his son-in-law, he suddenly hated Venezuela as a whole.

Six weeks after her nocturnal adventure, Gaby confessed to her father that she was pregnant.

One morning early, he said to Han and Ingrid: 'Now I'm going to show the two of you something I've kept a secret from everyone all these years, even my best friends.' They took the jeep until they were past Canaima, then a big canoe to the Yudi rapids, where they climbed into a smaller canoe that was waiting for them – Rudy had prepared this outing carefully.

They came past a sandbank where a few caymans were basking in the sun. Rudy jumped into the water and grabbed one of the *babas* right behind its head, so the animal was completely helpless. After the next bend in the river, four otters slid from the bank into the water, and Han almost couldn't believe his eyes. 'They're the size of seals,' he shouted, peering through the binoculars.

Around noontime they went on land, and walked for a while through the forest; Rudy told them about the expedition he had made years ago with a pair of British scientists along the Ahonda, a river whose headwaters he had never visited before. The deeper the expedition went into the canyon, the more wildly the Ahonda had twisted and turned, and with every bend in the river the rocks had grown taller, forcing them to portage the canoe all the time. The last bit they did on foot. Rudy walked out in front, and one of the Indians walked behind him; on his feet, that Indian was wearing something that was entirely new to the area at that time: shiny black shoes. Every time they had to cross a bit of mud or water, the Indian would take off those shiny black shoes, so they wouldn't lose their sheen. Just as they passed a couple of boulders, a bushmaster suddenly slithered past the man's shoes. The snake made two holes in the leather; Rudy had spun around, swung his machete, and, before the Indian even realized what was happening, the bushmaster had lost its head.

Now they crossed a river where a few Indians were picking fish out of the water, and Rudy explained it to them: during the dry season, the Indians dam off parts of the river with leaves and sticks and throw *barbasco* into it, a poisonous bark that paralyzes the fishes' gills. It's a fast way to catch fish, and a dangerous one; as long as the fish is cooked or roasted, the *barbasco* is not harmful to humans, not unless the person eating it has, for example, a cut inside his mouth. In direct contact with the bloodstream, the poison causes terrible hemorrhaging. Pregnant women have only to take a few sips of water poisoned with *barbasco* to be sure of a miscarriage. One afternoon – he didn't have his own plane at the time – a canoe pulled up to the shore at Ucaima, carrying a woman who was bleeding to death. He gave her an injection, administered a massive dose of vitamin K to slow the bleeding, and called for a plane. Two days later a Cessna landed in the field behind the camp; it was touch and go, but the woman had survived.

A hundred metres further along, he picked a nut from a bush. 'Tastes absolutely wonderful,' he told them. 'The loveliest nut you'll ever eat, but tomorrow your hair will fall out and it will take three months for it to start growing back. The forbidden fruit! The Pemón call it *cocodimono*, which means: "Don't eat it!" The weird thing is, some nuts are poisonous and others aren't, and it depends on the soil the bush grows in. No one has ever done research on how that works. I told a young botanist that once, told him it would be a great topic for his dissertation.'

After a good hour's walk, they came to a settlement. Rudy went into a hut, bowed deeply before an old Indian woman, took both her hands in his and said to Han: 'This is my real mother.' Han thought he was joking, and without paying it much heed he asked Rudy what her name was. Rudy said: 'Lola Castro.'

They gathered around the pot on the fire. It contained fish and meat and pepper; Han took a bite and almost spat it out right away. Rudy thought it tasted even better than the hotchpotch back in Holland.

Four or five huts further, as Han recalled; a little way along was an old man braiding a rope; the children came to Rudy to show him their sores– he had brought iodine and bandages with him, the way he always did when he went into the interior, and he cleaned their festering wounds. It was obvious to Han that the Pemón saw Rudy as a doctor. A young man came back from hunting; his name was Jésus. He was a handsome fellow, and Rudy said to Han: 'Whenever Jésus appears, it's time to lock up your daughters.'

Rudy hadn't felt like leaving, he just sat there talking, and he kept taking hold of old Lola's hand. Only at the end of the afternoon did he finally stand up. They took the final stretch of river in the dark, with Rudy shouting out above the roar of the outboard: 'A mother, Han, she treated me like a mother. Jesus, man, we didn't even know what a mother was, did we?'

The next evening, two men had come limping up onto the lawn at Ucaima. Their faces spoke of brawls fought with broken bottles, of months of wading through rivers under a pounding sun, of the kind of fever that leaves a yellow tint to your skin, of fleeting contacts with women who were in little better shape themselves, and of a smidgeon of hope and litres of rum and the ongoing hangover called loneliness. They had untied a handkerchief and showed Rudy the contents: Rudy called Gerti over, and together they picked out a couple of stones. The men seemed to come alive again once they had the banknotes in their hands, and they actually seemed in a hurry as they paddled off in their canoe.

There are some things you don't ask your brother. Such as: where did you get the money to buy a generator, a jeep, a plane? How did you pay for the building materials for a camp that, to hear you tell it, cost a million guilders? When you haven't seen that brother for twenty-eight years, you keep those questions to yourself. Especially when it's your youngest brother, who will tell you to mind your own damned business if he hears even the slightest suspicion in your voice. So Han told himself that it was none of his damned business, and merely whispered in Ingrid's ear on occasion: 'How did he ever pay for all this?' Han was familiar with Rudy's finances, or at least the official ones, and he knew that the expeditions didn't bring in a whole lot of money. What's more, Rudy was choosy about his guests; just a few days earlier he had turned away three Japanese tourists, even though there was plenty of room in the camp. Han had been unable to contain himself, and did the addition so that Rudy could see how many dollars he had missed with his rude refusal. But Rudy had calmly explained that he had no desire to spend three days in a boat with people with whom he couldn't speak a single word. 'They don't speak English, they don't speak Spanish, they use their cameras instead of their tongues, and they go around bowing and scraping. How would *you* like to spend your time with them?'

But after the visit by the *gareimperos*, it began to dawn on Han a little. Men like that couldn't be bothered to travel back and forth to the capital, they probably didn't have enough cash to pay for the trip, and besides, years of loneliness had alienated them from every living soul. Rudy, on the other hand, flew to Carácas regularly, and Gerti still had enough contacts from her years in the diamond export business to be able to sell the stones. It must have been a lucrative little operation, although Han could only guess how much his brother earned with it. For that was one area in which Rudy hadn't changed a bit: according to him, money was to be made however you needed to make it, but it wasn't something you talked about.

No, they spoke of other things, of life in the bush – Rudy's hobbyhorse.

'What you mean when you say 'jungle',' he preached during their trip to the Mayupa rapids, 'isn't the real jungle. Indifference is the real jungle.'

At the end of that same afternoon they arrived back at Ucaima; from the water you could barely see the buildings, most of which were hidden behind trees and bushes and hedges so full of flowers that dozens of hummingbirds swarmed around them.

'Paradise,' Rudy said, 'originally wasn't the same as the hereafter, that's what the Christians made of it. The word comes from the old Persian, *pairi-daéza*, which means a walled park or a garden with bushes around it. That's also where the late Babylonian *pardisu* comes from, and the Hebrew *pardes* and the Greek *paradeisos*. In all those languages, it refers to a place of peace and quiet. You find that back in the Garden of Eden, a garden between two rivers, the Tigris and the Euphrates, or,' he said with a grin, 'the Orinoco and the Amazon.'

'Far from Albertinestraat, in any case,' Han mumbled.

'You need to have enough space for it, of course, and the freedom, but not much more than that. Everyone can make his own *pairi-daéza*, everyone who wants to, but you have to be willing to work for it, not skimp on things, not go crying to the doctor every time it hurts a little, not give up the fight right away when things get difficult – and above all, not think that paradise is the same thing as sitting on your ass. Believe me, it's because of laziness that most people never find paradise, because of fear, pettiness, or because they're too easily satisfied with what they've got.'

But when Gaby got involved with the wood gnome, Rudy panicked. He had neglected or forgotten to show his children the other world, the world of streets, squares, palaces and cathedrals. He took Gaby along to Italy and Salzburg, he took Sabine to Spain and to Paris, he took Lily and Raúl along to Holland, to The Hague and to Naarden, but it was too late. Although they spoke German fluently, the girls weren't interested in Europe at all, and Sabine became involved with a Venezuelan as well, with Armando, who worked as a guide for the Canaima camp. It was another setback for Rudy. Armando was taller than Juan at least, and when he introduced himself as Armando Tovar, the conversation always turned quickly to the homerun which his father had once commented on with such a deluge of metaphors that traffic throughout Carácas had come to a halt. Armando was the son of the baseball commentator on Venezuelan national radio, and – because baseball, for most Venezuelans, is a kind of ritual, one to which they surrender with more verve than to any other faith – Tovar's voice had more authority for them than that of their father confessor. But Rudy soon discovered that Armando lacked his father's eloquence, and his nimble-mindedness, and his humour, that he had never read a book, never thought about anything longer than five minutes, that although he could mix a cocktail with his eyes closed, he had never heard of Mozart. And this was the man with whom he would be stuck at the camp for years to come, because of course he didn't have a decent job, and the only thing he wasn't shy about was bellying up to someone else's table.

Rudy had gone off to find a new kind of grandeur in the wilderness, and while he was sitting in a canoe with Prime Minister Trudeau or with Neil Armstrong, David Rockefeller or Prince Bernhard, he felt that he had succeeded at that quite well. Until one of his daughters married a backwoods hick, his other daughter a ninny, and the only son-in-law he really liked went and died.

Raúl Serrano died the death all bush pilots meet sooner or later: he crashed. He wasn't flying himself at the time: he was with two colleagues who wanted to demonstrate to him what the new twin-prop helicopter could do: they shut down one of the props, at too low an altitude, and the chopper landed on the rocks.

Lily never got over it: her first child – a boy – had been born only six weeks earlier. She and little Rudolf moved to Carácas, and rarely returned to the jungle.

I **had** the feeling there was another reason why Rudy had suddenly hopped on a plane in the late 1970s and flown to the Netherlands, where he stayed for a whole month in the country he had always claimed that he missed like a hole in the head. It would be a reason which explained why he told no one, not even his brothers, even though they were the only ones in whom he occasionally confided his innermost feelings. It was more than a suspicion: one source in particular made me quite sure that the real reason for his visit was to re-establish contact with Els.

In the boxes of correspondence at Ucaima, amid hundreds of Christmas cards, expressions of thanks and congratulatory telegrams, I found a bulging envelope with CONFIDENTIAL written on it in big letters, which of course piqued my curiosity.

The letter from Els was written on September 6th, 1979, after she had received two tapes from Rudy; one which he had recorded in his home, with music in the background, the other made during a trip to Angel Falls. Rudy was unable to write to her; he cramped up when he had a pen in his hand; he had to tell, and a cassette recorder got it all, his voice, the music and the soft rustling of the water. He chose the night as the time for his confessions, and with the cry of a startled bird as introduction he made a final attempt to talk Els into starting a new life, with him.

They had met ten years earlier; Els was twenty-three at the time, Rudy forty-one. It was in May of 1969, and she had been reluctant about flying to the Gran Sabana. Even in Carácas she was barely able to escape the little Shell clique, and to spend an entire weekend with her husband's colleagues and their wives felt like a punishment to her.

Then, suddenly, she found herself sitting across from a beanpole in khaki who told her that he had once survived for weeks on nothing but ants, who looked at her and held her gaze, who took a deep drag on his cigarette and said: 'You know what? You have beautiful eyes.' After which he got up, put a tape in the recorder, turned up the volume and asked her to dance. A slow, jazzy number; he kept a little distance between them, it's true, but his eyes never let her go. During the next song he pulled her carefully to him, during the third number the others decided it was high time to get some sleep, and her husband decided to go for a swim in the river. She remained behind with Rudy, at the bar, and he had barely poured her a drink when the lights went out. Later he confessed to her that he had set the timer on the generator to turn itself off at midnight; when he took her into his arms, it was premeditated.

There hadn't been enough room at Rudy's camp to accommodate the whole party; she and her husband had to sleep in hammocks. It was hard for her to fall asleep while rocking, she barely slept a wink. At the crack of dawn, she got up. Rudy was already up, he poured her a cup of coffee, then asked her not to go along with the rest of the group that day. Trips like the one they'd be taking today were nothing for him, he'd send an Indian along with them, and stay at the camp himself. When her husband and his colleagues appeared at the breakfast table, Els complained that her digestion was acting up and that it was probably better if she didn't go along. The group left, and in the shadow of a tree Rudy confessed to her that he could no longer stand being stuck at Ucaima with a wife who had become a complete recluse. 'Maybe you're the reason she's that way,' she tossed back at him. He didn't deny it; the way things had gone had made her withdraw even further into her shell, the first years had been hard and lonely, and, it was true, when there were guests he claimed all the attention for himself. He understood it, he just couldn't accept it. She'd become a stranger to him, and if it hadn't been for the children he would have left her long ago. He was crazy about his daughters, especially the youngest, '*mi conejo*' he smiled, 'my little rabbit'. Els looked him over carefully, and became increasingly impressed by his openheartedness. She helped him prepare for the evening meal, and in the early twilight they made love, on a flat stone along the riverbank.

The group left the next morning. At the bottom of the stairs to the plane, Rudy collected the business cards and nodded politely to everyone who invited him to come by next time he was in Carácas. He had told Els that he never accepted invitations like that, that whenever he was in Carácas he stayed with an old friend, the photographer George Steinheil. He had met Steinheil through Charlie Baughan, and the two of them spent whole nights reminiscing about back when they had studied maps together and drawn routes along rivers that had never been explored. It would be senseless, Els thought, to give him my address.

A few days later, there he was on her doorstep, yawning constantly and asking her for a cup of coffee – he'd spent the night in his car in front of her house. If she had felt any resistance until then, he had now won her over once and for

Rudy and Lupé in 1990
(photo: O. Hendriksz)

Francisco Monte de Oca and Olaf Hendriksz
(photo: J. Brokken)

One of the crypts
(photo: O. Hendriksz)

The anaconda
(photo: O. Hendriksz)

The Wei Tepui, from the air
(photo: O. Hendriksz)

Victorino Manrique (l.) and Antonio Monte
(photo: J. Brokken)

Victorino Manrique's *conuco*
(photo: J. Brokken)

One of the petroglyphs
(photo: O. Hendriksz)

Olaf Hendriksz and the bushmaster in the cave
(photo: J. Brokken)

Victorino Manrique's *conuco* after the fire
(photo: J. Brokken)

Olaf Hendriksz
(photo: J. Brokken)

Rudy Truffino, 1993
(photo: R. Truffino archives)

all; his cheerfulness was contagious, and his boundless energy made her once again feel as young as she really was.

Before long he was visiting her regularly, and when she asked him what it was exactly that he was looking for with her, he said: 'Warmth.' Besides, they came from the same country. 'I understand you,' he said. 'You and I have the same mentality.' And she understood that too, because she not only lived abroad but was also married to a foreigner who always wondered why Dutch people spoke so highly of that brand of cosiness which they call '*gezelligheid*'.

She accompanied Rudy to business lunches, where he either told stories or fell asleep; she did some of his purchasing for Ucaima. He showed her a different Carácas, he took her to the Botanical Institute, introduced her to Dunsterville, and drove her to the grubby Spanish taverna on a back street where he usually ate, where the customers pounded their fists on the table to get the waiters' attention. After a few bites he put down his knife and fork; he caressed her arm, and she thought he was the gentlest man in the world.

Not that he was the perfect lover; even when he lay in her arms, he was still restless; the haste had burrowed its way deep into his soul, and even after a furious bout of lovemaking he would hop into his clothes and leave, after giving her a quick kiss, for no clear reason and mostly because that's how he had left places all his life. But half an hour later he would be on the phone, telling her he'd never felt more wonderful and that he had no intention of wiping her lipstick off his cheek.

One day she went with him when he emptied his post office box: he simply stuffed all the letters into a garbage bag. He hated writing, and people who asked for information about a trip to Angel Falls of the Auyán Tepui never received a reply. Els offered to handle his correspondence, and to promote Ucaima. From that moment on they talked on the radio on an almost daily basis, and he involved her in his plans to organize expeditions with the British bush pilot Harry Gibson and the Dutch photographer Frans Kortenaar, expeditions that would go even deeper into the Gran Sabana. Gibson was the pilot who had made the dangerous dive into one of the holes of the Sarisariñama in 1964, thereby making him in Truffino's eyes the ideal man to explore the central and southernmost *tepuis*, while Frans Kortenaar, who had been living in Venezuela for the past twenty-five years, could do photo reports on the first expeditions. But the three men soon had a falling out; according to Truffino, because Kortenaar had his eye on Els. Gibson died in a crash a few years later.

In 1971, Els's husband was transferred to England. Rudy swore to her that their parting wasn't final, but never got in touch with her in the years that followed. Only six years later did he see Els again, when she visited her sister on Curaçao and flew on to Carácas a few days later. Then, too, a great many promises were made, but in the years that followed Rudy once again failed to write or call her even once.

In 1979, Els heard that Rudy was coming to the Netherlands to give a lecture at the Pulchri Studios in The Hague, the very same private club where his father used to seek the company of painters and playwrights after his work at the bank. Els assumed what I later came to suspect as well: Rudy was going back to Holland primarily to get in contact with her. Without informing him beforehand, she decided to attend that lecture, along with her husband.

Rudy was not only surprised, he was completely overwhelmed. Only with the greatest of difficulty was he able to finish reading his text. He had barely spoken the last lyrical line about the Gran Sabana when he rushed to Els, took her in his arms, burst into tears, sobbing on her shoulder like a little boy and stammering while all could hear that he loved her and that this time he would never let her go. For Els it was an embarrassing situation, although she knew it was just like Rudy to forget that there were two hundred people standing around. When he finally did realize that, he wasn't embarrassed at all: he had done as the spirit moved him, and he'd been precisely that uninhibited all his life.

'Your enthusiasm made me timid,' she wrote in her letter of September 9. 'I didn't know how to react, but what I realized in any event is that my feelings for you are deeper than I've ever been willing to admit to myself.'

The next day he and his brother Han left for Switzerland, to arrange some business matters. As soon as he got back to Holland, he contacted Els right away. 'Those were a few wild weeks,' she wrote to him later, obviously still a bit dazed.

Time and time again he declared his love to her; he asked her to come with him to Venezuela. When she replied that she thought the Gran Sabana was wonderful, but not as a place to which she wanted to disappear forever, he offered to buy her an apartment in Carácas. He would leave the camp to Gerti and a couple of experienced guides, and would only go back to the Gran Sabana for the bigger expeditions. Els didn't take him up on it; she didn't want to leave her children behind, and she couldn't imagine moving to Carácas with two boys who still had to start high school. After the nine years she had spent in Venezuela and England, she was finally back in her own country, and she didn't feel much like leaving right away again. Another reason was that Rudy was a Don Juan, and even if you found that charming about him, living with a Don Juan would definitely place constant demands on your own self-respect.

The moment came for him to go back to Venezuela. On the day he left, he wept without stopping. He said it was 'God-awful' that he had to go back, he found it 'God-awful' to be locked up with Gerti at the camp for months on end. Els brought him to Schiphol Airport, and even there he couldn't keep his sorrow under control. He refused to board the plane, he refused to show his passport, and finally two stewardesses had to pull him away from Els. Once the stewardesses had piloted him through customs, he turned around one last time and yelled: 'Els, I love you, you'll always be the only one in my life.'

Els ten Houte de Lange described to me in writing the scene he'd made, after I had written to her to ask a few questions. As it turned out, she still lived at the same address. The tone of her reply was a great deal more down-to-earth than the letter she had written nineteen years earlier, except when she wrote about their parting. 'He knew then,' she wrote, 'that we would never see each other again. It was just as painful for me. I loved him with all my heart, he was original, he had a hungry mind, a fantastic sense of humour, he was a wonderful raconteur and everyone was interested in what he said. He had a tendency to exaggerate, that's true, but once you saw through that he was an extremely sensitive and emotional man. But no matter how I admired him, I felt I had to choose for my children.'

When Rudy got back to Venezuela, he made one last attempt to change Els's mind. He sent her two tapes, and when she heard his voice on the tape, she was 'all broken up' and 'felt like running off and hopping on a plane to Carácas.' The first tape in particular went straight to her heart, 'as sad as you sound there, that's still the way I feel too, and I'm glad it's mutual.'

That first tape he had recorded with the sweet-voiced 'Bright Eyes' playing in the background, the song they had listened to so often. Tears came to her eyes as she heard him talk about their parting, with Art Garfunkel's voice in the background. 'Oh Rudy,' she wrote in her letter of September 9th, 1979, 'I long for you so desperately, what am I going to do without you! You say it's difficult to get over it, the same goes for me. I often ask myself why it is that we met again after such a long time and why everything between us was just the way it had always been, as though there hadn't been all those years in between: that everything just fell into place must have a meaning, or, what I'm really trying to say, must have a reason. I've gone through a fair amount in this area in my life, and so have you, but what we have between us is something you only experience once or twice in your life.'

She had experienced only rare moments of happiness with her husband, but he was the father of her children, and she had resigned herself to her life with him. Until she saw Rudy again: from that moment on, she was at a loss. She would hop in the car, drive down the same roads she'd driven down with him; she burned the dinner, ran out of the kitchen, collapsed in a chair in the garden and sat there for an hour, asking herself why he wasn't here or she wasn't there. She went to visit Rudy's mother, was annoyed at the negative way she spoke about him, couldn't believe that a mother would talk about her own son with such disdain. She apologized for having asked him questions about his childhood, about that girlfriend of his back then in the Noordoost Polder, about that other woman with whom he'd had an affair in the Netherlands; she knew he preferred not to talk about his younger years, and promised she wouldn't bring it up again.

On the tapes he sent, Rudy withdrew his earlier offer to

buy her an apartment in Carácas. Perhaps it would be better if she came and lived with him at Ucaima. Life in the jungle wouldn't be easy for her, and that had as much to do with the surroundings as it did with him. 'I'm no angel,' he admitted, with the rustling of the waterfall in the background, 'but I'm no devil either.' He asked whether she wasn't daunted by the idea of taking over the care for his three children, for although the oldest was already married and the other two were approaching twenty, they still acted like adolescents. 'No,' she answered him. 'But then, things haven't reached that point, and I wonder whether they ever will.'

Indeed, they never did. One year later she and her family were sent to the Middle East, three years later to Nigeria. When she wrote to Rudy, she foresaw that the distance between them would only become greater; at the same time, she realized that 'something is gone from my life that I miss intensely, and that thing is you.' At the end of her seven page letter she fantasized, spent the night with him at Angel Falls, and imagined how he would help her to pull off her tight jeans. That was the only sexual allusion she made: the letter is primarily about disappointments; they loved each other, they still love each other, but they are both trapped in their own lives.

In the final paragraph she drives her Volvo to the North Sea dunes, pushes Rudy's cassette into the tape player and listens in the dark to his voice, with 'Bright Eyes' in the background.

'I'll keep my eyes burning only for you, although they can become suddenly very pale, when I think of you so far away.'

Rudy took a canoe up the Orinoco; travelling had always been the best way for him to forget.

Gerti fled to places where she could relax. First she spent a few weeks on Margarita; in the following years she went to Martinique and Guadeloupe.

Back at Ucaima, however, she felt as tired as she had before she left. As soon as she had served dinner in the evening, she would go straight to bed, without eating a bite herself. For months she ignored the symptoms, for months she fought for every step she took; she allowed herself no weaknesses, because she had to keep the camp running. But when she started to faint constantly while standing at the stove, she realized that it was a losing battle, and that she could do nothing more to help the guests.

She went back to where she was born. In Salzburg she had an operation: it turned out she had a tumor in her head. She moved in her with her brother and sister-in-law and had to undergo radiation therapy twice a week. There was no longer any hope of a cure, but she was strong, and it took eight months for the illness to finally bring her to her knees.

In early May she began declining rapidly. Her brother sent a telegram to Ucaima, Rudy flew to Holland, and he and Han drove together to Salzburg. The reception there was cool; Rudy and Han had to sleep on a rug on the floor, which both of them experienced as a rebuke. One week later, Han had to return to Naarden on business; on June 3rd, when news came that Gerti had died, he drove back to Salzburg, this time together with Ingrid. The next day he picked up the Truffino girls at the airport; to his dismay, Lily, Gaby and Sabine began fighting almost right away.

During the early months of 1985, the daughters had taken turns coming to Salzburg to be with their mother. But when Gerti died, all three of them were back in Venezuela. Two days after her death they arrived in Salzburg. The tiring trip was probably partly to blame for their flying at each other so soon after arrival, perhaps sorrow had also made them defiant: when one's mother dies in her mid-fifties, it is not something one accepts as the hand of fate. Moreover, the bond between the three sisters had never been particularly strong; when they looked for support, they rarely turned to each other. But despite all mitigating circumstances, their haggling over the inheritance in the presence of their aunts and uncles, so shortly after arrival in Salzburg, did bear witness to a certain callousness of spirit. Rudy sat there cringing like a whipped pup. What he had suspected for a long time was now being confirmed; the years in the jungle, and their equally self-centred existence at the boarding school, had taught his daughters to look after themselves, but no one had ever shown them what affection meant. When he brought Gerti to her grave, therefore, he looked back on a double defeat; he had failed, both as a husband and a father. To Han he hinted that the former failure was something he regretted more than the latter.

'I couldn't get along with Gerti,' he told his brother after the funeral, 'but I never admired anyone the way I admired her.'

Back at Ucaima, Rudy let the phone ring and stopped answering all summons on the ultrashortwave radio. He planned to receive no guests for the next year. He lay in his hammock smoking like a fiend, spent entire days listening to Mozart's *Requiem*, and would then order the Castro brothers to prepare the *curiare*. The boat filled with cans of gasoline, they would head upriver, with no clear destination. Rudy sat motionless in the middle of the boat, his felt hat down far over his forehead, while the grim walls of the Auyán Tepui slid past. When the sun had gone behind the mountain he would pick out a sandy beach, build a fire and tie his hammock between two trees. Then he spent the whole evening staring into the fire, without saying a word. He, the talker, was silent, and it wasn't until the next morning that he spoke another word; he would say to the Castros: 'We're going,' and although it was not their custom to follow orders, they would fill the gas tank on the outboard and gather their things, knowing that this was not the time for objections. In fact, their boss was doing the same thing they did whenever life showed its darkest side: he was cutting himself off.

A year went by.

In the second year he led a few groups to the waterfall, but without much conviction.

Then he went to Carácas, and came back a few weeks later with Milagros. She was gorgeous; a full-blooded Italian right down to her bright-red fingernails, and she hit the whisky hard each night. Meanwhile, Gaby and Sabine ran the camp, and could have killed Milagros. She lorded it over them, had breakfast when it was already time for lunch, never carried a cup to the kitchen herself and was too lazy to put her own ice in her glass. The only reason she could have followed Rudy to Ucaima was his money: the daughters imagined their inheritance dwindling. Either she goes or we go, that was the tenor of the arguments, their father screaming that he had never in his life allowed anyone to tell him what to do, not even their late, beloved mother; Gaby and Sabine refused to budge, and in the end Milagros caught a plane back to Carácas.

One month later Rudy celebrated his sixtieth birthday; Lily, Gaby and Sabine had invited his oldest friends, and Aleksander Laime, and Anyatoli, and the Castros, and the Indians from the nearby *conucos*, eighty guests in all. The party lasted three days; one week later, the Indians were still half-tipsy. For the music, the girls had brought in the best *harpa* players of the llanos, for that was Rudy's new obsession: he collected music from all over Venezuela, and later on from all over South America, and finally from Africa and Southern Europe as well. When there were guests who bored him (and more and more guests seemed to do that), he would shout: 'And now we're going to take a little trip round the world! Music!' Then he would play ten or fifteen tapes back-to-back, and he would end the musical *tour d'horizon* with Símon Díaz. When Símon Díaz sang, he would close his eyes and murmur: 'Now *that* is authentic.'

It didn't happen very often anymore, but occasionally someone would come to Ucaima in whom Truffino saw a glimmer of himself.

He and Werner Herzog shared a fascination for desolate areas. In the late 1980s, the German film director spent a week in the Gran Sabana, and during their all-night conversations Truffino heard about Fitzcarraldo, the Irish adventurer who had gotten it into his head to build an opera house in the Amazon jungle, where Enrico Caruso would sing on the opening night.

It had taken Herzog five years to film Fitzcarraldo's life, and during the production he had encountered the same obstacles as his hero, who had begun on his megalomaniacal plan shortly before the turn of the 20th century. With his crew, Herzog went into the jungles of Peru, where he had made a movie once before, the conquistador epic *Aguirre*. To get around the impassable rapids, he had to have a steamboat pulled over a mountain by hundreds of Indians, and that boat was many times heavier than the one Fitzcarraldo had dragged from one river to the next. Just to get the ship up the forty degree slope was a titanic job in itself; even more difficult was to let it slide down the other side. Indian extras complained to German journalists about mistreatment. Herzog denied the allegations, but shortly afterwards the Indian bearers burned down the set; leading man Klaus Kinski told the director halfway through the film that he was going home, and Herzog could only keep him from doing so by pointing a pistol at him.

Truffino heard the stories and understood; this man had gone all the way to achieve his dreams.

In thanks for his trip to Angel Falls, Herzog sent him a tape with the musical score of the film, and from that moment on the voice of Caruso resounded regularly through the jungle around Ucaima.

One afternoon in autumn, Rudy showed up at the door again in Naarden. This time it was Han who let him in. Rudy hadn't really kept in touch since Gerti died.

Rudy had grown much older, and he seemed nervous. The thinning hair and the grey stubble didn't really surprise Han, but that his brother lit up a cigarette even before saying hello was something he found unfitting for a Truffino. Just like ten years earlier, Rudy had told the taxi to wait in the drive. When

Han came out to help his brother with the luggage, he saw a young woman in the back of the cab.

Rudy waved, the door opened, and Han noted that the woman who climbed out was not very tall or broad in the hips, that her hair was a lustrous black and gleamed even in the dull autumn light, and that her skin was brown, yellowish-brown. An Indian.

'Pemón?' he asked.

'No...' Rudy coughed heavily. 'Lupé's from Peru.'

That very same evening, Han said to Rudy: 'Too bad you didn't meet her a long time ago.' And Rudy leaned back in his chair and breathed freely at last – after all, you never know how your family will react.

Lupé got along reasonably well in English, and didn't have to hear a joke before laughing. Han found it peculiar that she addressed Rudy as 'Don Rudy', but then she came from a different world, and they were years apart. Exactly how she had arrived in Canaima was never really clear to Han. She had been with a man, from whom she was soon separated; in any case, as his brother put it: they fool around something fierce, there in Venezuela...

The two of them stayed in Naarden for a week, then Rudy took Lupé off to see almost every capital city on the old continent. The next year the roles were reversed: she guided him around Peru.

In 1992, Han and Ingrid went back to Ucaima. Alarming changes had taken place in the ten years since their last visit. While they were moving their things into Rudy's lodge at Angel Falls, a group of about thirty tourists landed across the river; the banks of the Río Churún were littered everywhere with cans and bottles and pieces of plastic. Rudy hadn't gone with them on that trip, he avoided Angels Falls as much as possible these days. The tourism, he told Han glumly, was ruining everything; the plants and animals suffered under it, the Pemón were leaving the savanna to move into hovels close to the Avensa hotel at Canaima, where the girls tried to seduce the guests and the men turned to drink. It was, in a certain sense, his own fault, and in order not to be reminded of that all too often he stuck more closely to home and spent his days reading. He asked himself questions. By consulting Heinrich Harrer, who had spent time with the Xingu Indians in the Amazon, or Claude Lévi-Strauss, who had clearly despised travellers, pioneers and explorers, or – and why not? – Nietzsche, whose *Zarathustra* told of a philosopher who had withdrawn from the world, he sometimes found an answer.

From a magazine Han had brought with him, he tore out an interview with the German artist Joseph Beuys. 'Man,' he underlined, 'must reestablish contact with the earthly. With the animals, the plants, with nature and with the angels and spirits.' And in the journals of Henry David Thoreau, published in 1981, the following sentences, written on August 30, 1856, made him pause and consider: 'It is in vain to dream of wildness distant from ourselves. There is none such. It is the bog in our brains and bowels, the primitive vigor of Nature in us, that inspires that dream.' And: 'Our limbs indeed have room enough but it is our souls that rust in a corner. Let us migrate interiorly without intermission, and pitch our tent each day nearer the western horizon.'

Three days later, Han and Ingrid came back to Ucaima. They sat down at the dinner table, Lupé was wearing a white T-shirt, a denim dress, a red ribbon in her hair, and when Han looked at his brother he thought: 'He's finally found the peace he's been looking for all his life.' The stories started, Lupé encouraged her Don, Rudy took another sip, let the ice cubes tinkle in his glass and, when the bottle of rum was empty, said: 'Well, I think I'll go looking for my hammock.'

Before returning to his own house, Rudy took a little walk along the river with Lupé. Han followed them at a distance. His brother leaned heavily on Lupé, and paused for breath every four or five steps. Compared to him, Han noted, Rudy had lived life twice over, and now he was paying the toll. The man he saw walking away in the distance was an old man. Han knew that his brother didn't have much time left.

III

They spoke no lies

Olaf Hendriksz was waiting for me when I got off the plane at Canaima. I recognized him immediately amid the waiting crowd: he stood head and shoulders above the Venezuelans. When he came up to a me a few minutes later, his high black hiking boots made it look as though he had already started up a mesa. He talked me past the *Guardia Nacional*, tucked two thousand bolívar notes into the hand of another official, took my backpack, asked, after picking up my suitcase at the luggage terminal, whether I always took so much baggage with me when I travelled, and pointed out the truck that would take us to the river. We climbed into the open bed, he took off his black felt hat, shook a shower of sweat out of his hair and panted: 'You'd better get used to it quick, man; this is as hot as it's ever been here.'

This was how I had imagined Rudy Truffino would receive me in 1995, the first time I'd breathed the spicy air of the savannas.

Almost three years had gone by since then. After speaking to people in the Netherlands, I had decided to go back to the Gran Sabana to do more research in Truffino's library and archives, to talk to his daughters about what they remembered, to take a closer look at the most important locations in Rudy's life and, above all, to establish contact with the Pemón. I had gradually found out who Rudy Truffino was, I had travelled with him through time, but most of my informants were white, and I wanted to know how the Pemón saw him. Because of Truffino, or at least largely

175

because of him, a large portion of their territory had been opened up to the rest of the world. That area was then declared a national park, and as park director Truffino had successfully tripled the area of the park, so that the entire Gran Sabana now fell under strict conservation laws. What did that mean to the Pemón? I had hoped to meet Lola Castro, who had adopted Rudy as her son – and she had never left the deep forest, where she lived amid her tribespeople. Right before my departure, however, Olaf had let me know that Lola had died. But there was another person with whom I could speak, another Pemón who had known Rudy from the earliest days, who had made many trips with him to the top of the Auyán Tepui, who had accompanied the Dunstervilles on the big orchid expedition of 1963, and who, along with Rudy, had found the wreck of Jimmy Angel's plane. I had seen him mentioned before, in Dunsterville's report: his name was Francisco Monte de Oca.

For at least ten, perhaps even fifteen years, Monte had been part of the regular crew of Indians who did the heavy work during the expeditions Truffino organized. In the mid 1970s he had gotten his fill of carrying and climbing, and had gone back into the interior with his wife and children. Since then he had resumed the semi-nomadic life of the Pemón, regularly clearing a tract of forest, cultivating a few fields, building two or three huts and living there until the soil was depleted. 'I know how to find him,' Olaf's fax had said.

I met Olaf through Han Truffino. When Han arrived at the subject of his brother's final years, he said: 'Of course, Olaf could tell you a lot more about that period. He was almost a part of the family then, and Rudy more or less regarded him as his son.'

My first meetings with Olaf took place in Amsterdam. He

was in his mid-thirties, but when he looked at me from behind his steamy glasses with that ironic little smile of his, he seemed ten years younger. He couldn't sit still for long; he rarely finished an anecdote without getting up to look for a book or a photo, which always took him at least fifteen minutes; the apartment he was living in looked like a secondhand bookseller's. I saw him as a pleasantly erratic scatterbrain, but when it came right down to it, he assured me, he didn't panic easily.

Olaf Hendriksz's life, particularly his background and adolescence, displayed some striking parallels with Rudy's. His father was a bank manager as well, his parents had also divorced when he was about ten, and he too had seen a family fall apart. But by far the most important similarity was that Olaf, like Rudy, had been a problem child. He had been kicked out of three intermediate schools and four high schools; after going through them, he finally ended up at a prep school, which he completed. By the time he was finished, most of his friends were already at university; school, he said, had started becoming 'really boring'. Being conscripted into the army was a way out. Once in uniform, he started 'really raising hell'; fourteen months later he snuck off to Italy for a while, but his father made him come back to Holland and had him tested by a certain Professor Bladergroen, who found out what his father had known all along: his son was capable of successfully completing any course of study he chose. 'You see,' his father said, 'you just don't want to.' And indeed, besides having a good time, there wasn't much of anything he wanted to do. He worked for a real estate agency for a few months, then at a chemical factory, spent a few months at an ad agency, but only really felt satisfied once he'd started typing his letter of resignation.

From his earliest childhood, Olaf had been friends with Han and Ingrid Truffino's son. In Naarden he had already became well acquainted with the legend of 'the uncle in the jungle', about whom so many stories were told that he could barely believe them; in 1988, however, he met him in the flesh. Rudy listened to his story, grinned and said: 'You know what you should do? Head for the woods.' That sounded like a good idea to him; like Rudy, he was sick and tired of Holland, where the 'wheel-clamp mentaility' didn't even leave you enough room to turn around. After a huge farewell party, during which the beer flowed freely and his friends roared in chorus: 'Olaf, Olaf, Olaf of the Jungle!', he left for two years at Ucaima. The morning after his arrival he found a green snake rolled up in front of his door; Truffino's daughters began giving him a hard time right away, and after he had taken his first steps into the jungle, he had to admit that his father was right: nothing beats certainty. 'So they've got plenty of plastic here too,' he said at the end of that trip, whereupon Rudy advised him to step aside; he was standing on a coral snake. Within the next second he had decided to enjoy the jungle elsewhere; at home, for example, on the couch, in front of the TV. The only thing that kept him from really going back to Amsterdam was the grin on his friends' faces. 'Little too much for you, hey, Olaf?'

Rudy taught him to shoot rapids, showed him where you could go ashore safely and where you couldn't, taught him how to calculate the river's rise, which stars you needed to navigate by when you got lost, how to administer snakebite serum, where you had the best chance of finding a colony of squirrel monkeys, which parts of the Auyán Tepui you should avoid – the western part, because the surface there consists of little staffs of rock with razor-sharp tips – and then, of course, all about plants, trees, birds, ants, butterflies and fish. After the first year he sent Olaf with two Indians into the darkest part of the forest, south of the Auyán Tepui, to cut down a tree that could be hollowed out for a canoe. It was the test of his mastery. After he had made it back to Ucaima two weeks later with the tree trunk, he was allowed to take groups into the area himself. He guided dozens of them, primarily fresh-faced botanists who wanted to see with their own eyes the *tierra-firme* riverbanks and the carnivorous plants on and around the mesas. He learned Spanish; just like Rudy, however, he would continue to speak it like a truckdriver. He also learned Pemón, after he became involved with an Indian girl. He lived with her in a *conuco* for awhile, then left. Why? When I asked him that, he smiled insecurely for the first time. 'Aw, never mind.'

By the end of the second year, the Truffino girls had really started making him 'want to puke'; Sabine in particular proved to be 'a pain in the ass'. He didn't earn much, he was dependent on the tips he received, and when he found out that Sabine wasn't passing those along to him he threw in the towel. He told Rudy, 'Take your daughters and shove them up your ass,' and left. But two months later Rudy called him to say that he had 'thrown the whole damn family out of the house', and four months later Olaf was back. From 1990 on he spent nine months a year in Venezuela, led dozens of groups through the Gran Sabana, and later through the Orinoco and Amazon basins as well. After every tiring trip he returned to Amsterdam; two weeks later he would find himself putting on a video about the Gran Sabana, just to stay in the mood, and four weeks later he'd have had his fill of the musty air in the dilapidated house on the Ceintuurbaan. There was nothing new you could tell him about the lure of the rainforest.

After five afternoons of talking to him in Amsterdam, I asked whether he would accompany me to meet the Pemón. He didn't hesitate for a moment. 'I'd love to.' He could combine it with another trip, and he wanted no pay for the time we'd spend among the Pemón. 'I'm doing it for Rudy. Because I want to say that up front: I loved that man dearly.'

After I had systematically run through Truffino's archives and checked my old notes, we took the canoe up the Moroco, a narrow river that meanders in its lower reaches across the savanna and cuts straight through the jungle further up. Just like three years earlier, when I had gone with Josef Gregori to Orchid Island and Angel Falls, José Castro was steering the boat. Still bent over almost double beside the outboard, still wearing a red T-shirt and jeans; I had the impression that only a few days had passed since my last visit.

Josef was not with us, but I had seen him only the day before. He was just stepping into a *curiare* when I called out his name. He turned, thought for a moment, then remembered. 'Janito!' He had a crew cut these days, and his floppy ears were even more badly sunburned than they'd been on the trips we'd made together. He was doing well, that's right, Janito, very well, in fact it couldn't be better. Did I remember how he had been learning words from a book señor Rudy had given him? Japanese, that's right. Well, now he was putting the final hand to the preparations for a trip to Angel Falls with a Japanese TV crew. He asked whether I was staying at Rudy's camp again, and when I nodded he said: 'Things are going a lot better there.'

The reign of the spiders and the white ants was, indeed, a thing of the past. The buildings had been painted, the bushes pruned, the grass mown. All the work of Armando, who had truly taken command. Expeditions were leaving from Ucaima again, most of them by helicopter. No one was secretive about Rudy anymore; he had died, that's right, years ago, and anyone who wanted to honour his memory could put flowers on his grave.

Rudy had enjoyed travelling on the Moroco. It was so shallow that larger boats had to avoid it; the only vessels you encountered there were Pemón canoes. Whenever Rudy took his *curiare* up the river, he went back in time to his early years when he was the only white man among the Indians.

Moroco, José told me, meant 'fighting' in Pemón; legend had it that two families had once fought for the right to fish in this river – among the Pemón too, it seemed, peace and contentment also had their limits. Later, Francisco Monte gave us a different explanation for the river's name: moroco was derived from the Spanish *morocoto*, meaning 'coin'. Golden ducats had once been found in the river, left there after a boat full of Spanish soldiers had capsized. That sounded far-fetched to me. Or had the Spanish conquistadors actually gone much further up the rivers of the Gran Sabana than had been assumed? Not much research has been done into the history of the Guyanese interior; little is known about either its conquerors or its earliest inhabitants.

The day before, Olaf had taken me to see a few crypts on the savanna, dome-shaped graves of stone and mortar. The only building materials the Pemón use are wood and palm leaves; the mounds must have dated from pre-Columbian times. Had they been built by a native people with a more advanced culture? But if so, who were they? And when did they inhabit the Guyanese highlands? During one of his earlier visits, Olaf had removed some of the earth from around the crypts, and during every storm after that, lightning had struck their stones, even though they rose barely a metre above the tufts of grass. The Pemón explained their magnetic power by referring to the gold that was said to lie buried deep in the crypts; two Indians had once gone digging there, but on the way back their boat had turned over in the rapids and they had drowned. The accident came as absolutely no surprise to the Pemón: an Indian who failed to leave the dead to rest could count on the vengeance of the *canaima*. At the same time, however, a good deal of digging had been done around the crypts since Olaf's last visit.

The Moroco coiled through the same savanna where we had pulled away the grass around the crypts the afternoon before. Kingfishers flew out in front of the boat, skimming the water's surface. The Venezuelans call them 'fish-hunters', which explains their great numbers close to the river; we saw them in every shape and size.

We moved on beneath a cloud of white butterflies – no passing rainstorm could have cast a darker shadow on the river. The little waves thrown up by the bow of the boat rolled onto the sandy banks and splashed against the roots of the *moriche* palms; higher up along the banks we saw the *pulpo*– a tall, orangeish tree that is also referred to in Dutch as the 'octopus tree' – and a jacaranda with its purple flowers. *Herones* watched us motionlessly from their perches in the *pulpo*. Olaf, who was now paddling in the bow of the boat, shouted out the names to me, and I thought of Josef Gregori, whom Truffino had trained as well. Rudy must have been a good teacher; both men puttered about the Gran Sabana as though they'd been born there.

The river was full of rock shelves that the boat could just barely cross, as long as the outboard was lifted in time to keep the propeller from hitting stone. The greatest obstacles, however, were the fallen trees; they were sometimes hard to go around, and on two occasions we had to lift the boat over a half-decayed trunk. For the turtles, the fallen trees were the ideal place to sun; as soon as we approached their solarium they would drop into the water with a loud plop, and swim away hurriedly.

After a little more than an hour on the river, we reached the point Olaf had marked on his map. We climbed out of the canoe; José deemed it wiser to stay by the boat – passing Pemóns might otherwise take the outboard, assuming that anything left behind unguarded had no owner. The Venezuelans interpret that behaviour differently: they say the Pemón steal like magpies.

We followed the path through the jungle. *Grillos*, tree frogs, made a deafening noise, drowned out on occasion only by the shrilling of the *chicaras*. 'The circular saws among the crickets,' Olaf called them. The *pipi you* wailed straight through it all; when that bird squeezed its cry of *youyóuuu* out of its throat, it sounded like an air-raid siren going off. The further we got from the river, the more loudly the jungle manifested itself. When the shrieking and the stridulation would ease off for a moment, we could hear leaves rustling; unsettling, in light of the fact that there was not the slightest breath of wind.

For the time being, however, we were spared the unbearable, nauseating heat of which Von Humboldt and Bates regularly complained when they crossed the area between the Amazon and the Orinoco. The temperature of around thirty-four degrees that day may have been unusually high for the Gran Sabana, but it had not rained for months, and the air was not sweltering with humidity. Olaf found it reasonably easy going as well; during the rainy season, he said,

JAN BROKKEN

even thirty-degree heat was unbearable here.

Before reaching the *conuco* the path first climbed a few dozen metres; we were panting heavily by the time we said hello to Francisco Monte de Oca. He didn't seem at all surprised to see us appear out of the jungle; I saw a little twinkle in his eye, and he showed us right away to the hammocks hanging near the huts.

Olaf asked whether he had truly worked for Rudy Truffino.

'Djudy? *Claro que si*! For years!'

We slid the packs off our backs and dropped down into the hammocks. Francisco was wearing only a pair of trousers, which he could no longer button due to his sizeable paunch; he lay down in a hammock as well and folded his hands over his bare belly.

His wife came over. She was short, skinny and missing almost all her teeth. She greeted us, but only after ladling up a bowl of *cachiri* from a plastic tub.

'Don't drink too much of it,' Olaf warned, 'or you'll have to tie your pant legs closed around your ankles.'

Francisco's son joined us. The rodent Antonio was holding to his chest looked suspiciously like a rat, although its long whiskers made it look a bit friendlier. He lay petting the animal, then leaned over, picked up a few twigs and began whittling them with his two-edged knife into arrows with which he hoped to shoot a few fish later that afternoon. The little animal remained lying on his stomach like a kitten the whole time. Antonio's wife came over to say hello, an infant at her breast; four or five children crowded around us, the oldest no more than nine, all of them with dirty faces, all of them wearing faded T-shirts that were far too big for them. The T-shirts were full of rips and holes, and beneath them the children wore nothing at all.

'We've seen some hard times,' Francisco began.

'Tell us,' Olaf said.

'We lost our last dog.'

'Sick?'

'No, he was eaten by a tiger.'

The Pemón call all feline predators *tigres*, not just jaguars, but also the smaller ocelots or even smaller *margays*.

'Was it deep in the jungle?'

'No, close by. Less than five minutes from here.'

'And now you're frightened?'

Francisco grinned; that was a question only a white man would ask.

'Tigers don't attack people. Not unless they're incredibly hungry, and even then only if they've already eaten people. Then they remember the flavour.'

'But you can't tell that by looking at them.'

'No. So you take a light with you. Just shine it at them and they run away. Too bad about the dog, though. It was a good animal. The other *conucos* have been having the same problem. In the last couple of months, about thirty dogs have disappeared.'

'Why are the tigres so hungry?'

'The drought. The smaller game has gone further into the forest, and then the tigers have nothing to eat.'

Olaf talked about El Niño, but Francisco didn't really understand.

'You know,' he said at last, 'if a world war would break out, we would be the last ones to notice. If we even noticed…'

And that was my impression as well. Here there was only the chirping of the circular saws, and when you stretched your legs in a hammock beneath these trees, Europe and Asia and the United States were on a different planet.

We consulted with Francisco. Would it be possible for us to come back in a few days? Could we stay at his *conuco* for a week or so? Would he be willing to tell us about his experiences with Rudy Truffino, and the first expeditions to the Auyán Tepui? To all these questions Francisco nodded yes.

'Be sure to bring a few chickens with you, though; with this dry spell we're not able to shoot much game. We haven't eaten meat for a long time. And matches. And salt. And Polar. And dogs. Do you have dogs at Ucaima? Bring two of them with you, a *conuco* should have dogs.'

I thought about what I had read in Albert Helmans' history of Guyana: that the Indians were the first people to move in the company of dogs, during the hunt, during walks through the forest or when sitting on a stool in front of their hut.

There was only one thing that had irritated Francisco. We had asked him his age.

'I don't know. I don't care. I was born in January 1939. So figure it out for yourselves.'

We put on our packs again and started back. Francisco walked a little way with us. He panted heavily, and climbing the hill took all the strength he had. He rocked back and forth on his bowed legs to show us that he could hold his own, swung his machete forcefully to mow away branches blocking the path.

Before we said goodbye, he reached down and squeezed his thigh muscles.

'I'm not too fast anymore. I let Antonio do the hunting. But there's a few years in me yet.'

Age is hard to accept anywhere, but in the jungle, where life is a long and difficult search for food, a man who wobbles with every step he takes must feel useless indeed.

Olaf made the preparations for our stay in the jungle, drew up long lists of things we should absolutely not forget, looked in the sheds to find what Rudy had taken on his expeditions, inspected the ropes on the hammocks, sewed up the holes in the mosquito netting, sharpened the machete, went to the dispensary and found talcum powder, alcohol and mosquito repellent, pills for fevers and intestinal infections, antivenin for snakebites, and a recent invention, a little device used to draw the venom out of the wound immediately after a bite.

In the meantime, I talked to Gaby Truffino de Jiménez, who had come over for a week from Puerto Ordaz.

Gaby spent only one night at Ucaima, the others at the camp she and her husband had built a few kilometres north of Canaima, after the conflict over Lupé had reached a point where the screaming lasted for hours and the sullen silences for days, the latter being the most nerve-racking of all. The women who responded to Rudy's advances, Gaby felt, were only after his money. First she'd had to put up with Milagros, but when Lupé showed up she'd had enough. She turned her back on her father's camp and started for herself.

I could still hear the bitterness in her voice the morning she told me that, sitting on a bench in front of the simple shelter she and her husband had built. A little further away, Juan was building a bed from planks he had sawn from a treetrunk himself; across the yard, Gaby's two youngest sons were playing – the oldest of the three boys was helping his father. It had taken a great deal of persistence on my part before I was able to speak to Gaby; she kept coming up with excuses. Although she knew that I spent days nosing about in her father's archives, that never prompted her to ask exactly what I was planning to do. When I showed her the diary her mother had kept, she said: 'Oh yeah, I leafed through that once.' But she had never read it.

Gaby had a man's build. She was at least one metre eighty tall, had shoulders that could push a jeep out of the mud, arms that could lift a canoe out of the water, legs sturdy enough to climb a mountain, and short blonde hair with a reddish sheen in sunlight. The only friendly thing about her face were the freckles; her eyes, on the other hand, looked so worried that I wondered whether she ever smiled, and her lips curled upwards only when she said '*ach Quatsch*'. She spoke German flawlessly, with a slight Austrian accent; the German she had learned from her mother, in other words, who had always continued to speak her native language with Rudy and the three girls. Gaby must have resembled Gerti quite strongly; a hardworking woman with all the warmth of an ice cube. Not one of her recollections reflected any nostalgia whatsoever. At the end of the two conversations I had with her, I concluded that she would rather have grown up anywhere else, as long as it had nothing to do with incredibly beautiful Ucaima.

Her troubles really started the moment she took Juan in her arms, which must have been a rather comic sight, because he was three heads shorter than her. That didn't seem to matter to her, and she had married him before she was even fully grown. 'To get back at her father,' Olaf had once said to me, and it must have been Rudy who suggested that to him. For that is how Rudy saw it: she was trying to hurt her father's pride by taking up with that gnome. When I asked Gaby whether that had actually been at the back of her mind, she replied with '*quatsch*', but without really sounding annoyed. Her father, of course, had hoped she would marry someone more cultured, someone who had gone to school and earned good money, but where would she have met a man like that? She had attended a girls' boarding school with a regime as strict as a Prussian military academy; she was never allowed to go into town alone. During the holidays, she helped her mother, as a chambermaid. By the time she turned eighteen she was back in Ucaima– scrubbing toilets, cleaning the sheets, picking palm worms out of the butter, serving dinner, washing the dishes with river water that was too flat to get the grease off the plates. They had worked like crazy, not just her mother and father, the children too. A romance with one of the guests? Mutti and the girls were in the kitchen, peeling potatoes! Whenever she had a free moment she got out of there and went to Canaima. And who did she meet in Canaima? Boys like Juan: there weren't any others.

As a very little girl, she had played with Indian children. Her first language was German, her second Pemón. Not that that had brought her any closer to the Indians. They didn't live the way people like us lived, tomorrow was as far away to them as the next century; if they had something today, they finished it today; they just lived from one day to the next, they weren't interested in a good house or a good marriage; they just did whatever they felt like. No, she didn't have much feeling for the natives. Humans in their natural state, all right, but without the respect for nature that her mother and father used to have. She had forgotten most of her Pemón by now; she still understood a few words, but she never spoke it anymore.

Before they'd sent her to the German-language boarding school in Carácas, she had known nothing about the world; there was no telephone at Ucaima, they couldn't listen to the radio, there was no TV either, just a plane that flew in once a week, on Friday, and it left again on Monday. Sometimes the pilots came to the camp for a beer, and that was the only time she heard anything about the outside world. There was no time to read, no time to play either; even as a little girl she'd been expected to help out. Sometimes, when there were no guests, her father would pick out a little melody on the guitar, or teach his daughters a song. During the early days there was no money for a generator, so they had no electricity; if they wanted to hear music, they had to make it themselves. But there was always something breaking down at the camp, and her father always had to repair it himself; by the time he finally picked up his guitar again, lizards would come crawling out of the soundboard.

At the age of eleven she was already taking guests to the waterfalls; her father sometimes spent weeks on the Auyán Tepui, and her mother had to run the camp, so she and Lily would go out with the newcomers. The guests thought that was cute; they had the impression that they were visiting a whole family, right in the middle of the jungle, but they were never a real family. Her father and mother didn't get along; they may have respected each other, but they went completely mad when they had to spend time together. For her mother, life consisted of working. And when she wasn't working, she was thinking about all the work that still had to be done. Her father was more flexible, he would sit down at the bar to talk to the guests, but her mother considered that a waste of time. At ten o'clock at night her mother would still be hard at work; her father would shut the door behind him and read. In those days, the library was three times the size it was at the time he died– he gave away a lot of books. As far as that went, he had become a kind of Pemón, he wasn't attached to the things he owned, if he could make someone else happy with a book he had enjoyed himself, he was pleased. He was the same way with music: if people liked something they'd heard, he would dash off and copy a tape for them. He was a glutton for information, he wanted to know about everything and be able to talk about everything. People clung to his every word, especially the women. God, yes, he was a man who never bored you, who was always swept away by his own stories, and who couldn't help flirting. But he had no time for his children. When they had to go to boarding school, Lily and Sabine had felt that as a banishment; they had the impression that their father and mother had other things on their minds and were pleased to be rid of them. Gaby understood her parents' decision better; at the age of seven or eight they were still completely cut off from the world, they simply had to go to school.

Exactly where her parents came from originally, she had no idea. Sure, her father had told her about the bombardment. He'd had a lot of bad experiences, so many that he didn't like talking about the past. And her mother? Her mother never had time to talk about her younger years: she was working, always working. The first time Gaby had seen the Netherlands was in 1985. After her mother died, her father took her along to visit his family. Lots of rain, that was all she could remember, lots of rain, very cold. In Salzburg it had been even colder. Maybe her father had taken her with him to Europe another time as well, she didn't recall. She had stayed in Salzburg for three months (according to Han Truffino, it was three weeks), but the only thing she remembered about it was that her mother was dying, and that even then she hadn't been able to carry on a real conversation with her daughters. Oh yes, her mother had forgiven her for marrying Juan. That wasn't really necessary, though, because she had been much less opposed to the marriage than Rudy had. He had immediately started shouting 'Impossible!' and 'I won't have it!' During the final weeks of her mother's life, she had tried to show some warmth towards her children, but that had made her daughters so uncomfortable that she stopped soon enough. She couldn't make up in a few weeks for what she'd failed to do all her life; she had given up everything for Ucaima, and as a result she had become a stranger to both her husband and her children. The camp, or rather, the kind of life she wanted to lead, had made her a slave: the desire for freedom can also enslave you. Gaby had learned from that; she left the daily running of her own camp to Juan, spent only the school holidays at Canaima, and the rest of the year she was with her children, who went to school in Puerto Ordaz.

Lily never showed up. Olaf had asked her to come to Ucaima so I could talk to her about her recollections, but three times in a row she cancelled at the last moment. But it was all right with her if I stayed in her room, she told Olaf when she called from the capital; all the other rooms in the camp had since been taken, by a French biologist, an American geologist, and by Princess Beatriz Hohenlohe, whose father had fled from the Südetenland before the war and started with the development of the Spanish beach town of Marbella, which had made him incredibly rich. Beatriz Hohenlohe had landed at Ucaima with her daughter, her son-in-law, her two grandchildren and the pilot of her private jet. After she arrived, I had to look for another place to sleep.

It was to be Lily's room, in the far left wing of the camp compound. Since Lily had left, nothing had changed there; it was easy for me to imagine how she had spent her entire childhood in that room. It was right on the riverfront, and looked out on the mesas, the Nonoy Tepui, the Topochi Tepui, the Kuravaina Tepu and, in the distance, the mostly misty northern flank of the Auyán Tepui. Perfection is perhaps nowhere to be found, but to wake up every morning to a landscape like that had to make up for a great deal. The little sandy beach right below the window made it even more idyllic; here one could hop out of bed and dive right into the water. The bed was in front of the window, a wide bed that was still neatly made up, with the sheet turned back halfway. Lily had asked, however, if I would sleep in the other bed, the smaller one that belonged to her son. In the middle of the room was a hammock; against the left wall was a rattan bookcase, where I found a great many reference works about butterflies and reptiles. The ceiling was hung with fine-mesh nets; because of the high humidity, plasterwork here had a tendency to crumble; the nets also served to catch the lizards and ants that fell from the ceiling all the time. A sturdy breeze was blowing in through the screened window; the bows and arrows on the right wall and the curve in the back wall made me feel as though I were staying in an Indian hut. It seemed the kind of place where I could easily stay for weeks, until I woke up halfway through the first night with a terrible itch and discovered I was covered in fleabites.

I regretted Lily's unwillingness to talk to me. She must have been lot more like her father than Gaby was; her room was proof enough of that. I recalled what Olaf had told me once about Lily: one day her pet toucan had disappeared and in the nights that followed she prowled around the camp, looking for the murderer. Then, early one morning, she saw a *rabi pelado* pounce at a bird; from a distance, these opossums look like huge rats, but their tails are scaly and they have the head of a predator. (Shortly afterwards I was able to see this with my own eyes; an opossum had gnawed its way through the roof of the dining room, and one evening we found him hissing and spitting above our heads, baring his big, razor-sharp teeth.) Lily had grabbed the animal with her left hand and slashed its throat with the knife she carried in her right.

Gaby's memories were, I suspected, coloured by what had happened later. Her rather negative view of the Pemón must have come from the same source. After all, Juan had some Indian blood in him, although he always denied that, and she never tired of talking about what a hard worker Juan was, unlike the local natives. Lily suffered from no such frustrations, and I was sure she looked back on her youth with more pleasure, even though she had been the one most adamantly opposed to the arrival of Milagros, and could have drunk the blood of any woman who even spoke to Rudy.

Olaf, who had spent years with the family, called the three daughters 'white Indians' – introverted, too people-shy to communicate normally, frustrated in many ways. He thought Gaby was the most normal of the three, although she too was unpredictable, and he had always had to guess at her intentions.

Perhaps that was the only way it could have been. I myself would be unable to stick it out longer than three months in the jungle; from their earliest childhood, the Truffino sisters had put up with black scorpions, anacondas, coral snakes, huge adders, ants that could give you a twenty-four hour fever, wolf spiders and tarantulas, vampire bats, fleas, ticks, bedbugs, wasps and all manner and sizes of mosquito. And on their plates they found catfish full of bones, because sometimes there was nothing else to eat for days at a time. During the rainy season the river left its banks and the water sometimes rose so quickly that it entered their rooms and they would see their things floating away in the early morning light. For years they'd had to put up with the whims of nature, and there had been little fun to compensate for that. No girlfriends to whom they could air their feelings, no boyfriends with whom they could dance the salsa at parties they'd organized themselves, only guests who had to be pampered.

In the end, the daughters could no longer get along with each other or with their parents, and after yet another quarrel Rudy had sighed to Olaf: 'My family and I have nothing in common.'

At Francisco's *conuco*, the youngest child had fallen ill. When we arrived early in the afternoon, and went into the biggest hut to unload our packs, we found Florencia and Otilia bent over the hammock where the sick child slept. The little boy was coughing deeply; that morning he had awoken with his teeth chattering with fever.

Otilia let a pair of ants crawl across the child's skin, and with her index fingers she directed the insects from the arms to the chest and from the chest to the stomach. The child was too ill to feel the itching and the trail of bites the animals left on his skin. Meanwhile, Florencia murmured the charm she had learned from the shaman: Francisco asked whether he should go and fetch the *taren esak*, the sorcerer. Florencia decided to try something else first, rummaged around in a wicker basket, took out a little jar, opened it and shook out a few small grains of something onto her hand. 'Powdered snakeskin,' Olaf guessed. She opened the child's mouth and sprinkled his tongue with the pellets; the boy swallowed a few times.

It was, indeed, the pulverized skin of a rattlesnake which she had given the child. Because of the high humidity, the Indians in the jungle often have problems with infected or irritated airways. The shed skin of a snake they regard as the best cure for asthmatic complaints or bronchitis.

'And now we just have to wait,' Florencia said to Francisco.

Taking little, catlike steps, she went to hearth outside and came back in a minute with a cloth soaked in boiling water, which she laid on her grandson's forehead.

Francisco stayed away from the hammock. In order not to get in the women's way, he took us on a tour of the local hazards. Picking up a stick, he poked about amid the leaves of a tree in which a few wolf spiders lived. He had burnt out their nest a few times, but the spiders would not be discouraged; when he started sprinkling the petroleum around, they sought shelter elsewhere, only to return to the same spot a few hours later. The two dogs we had brought with us from Ucaima gave the tree a wide berth, and growled whenever they saw one of the hairy brown spiders appear from under the leaves. They knew what to look out for in the jungle, and they kept a respectful distance from those spiders.

On the other side of the *conuco* was a colony of pitch-black ants, the biggest ants I had ever seen, perhaps two centimetres long. These were the feared *veinte-cuatro* ants. When one of them bites you hard, on the foot for example, you are deathly ill for the next twenty-four hours. It had happened to Gaby once, Olaf told me: it started with vomiting and an unbearable headache, then everything went black and then she spent the next twenty-four hours in a coma. The next day she was able to get up again and could remember nothing of what had happened.

There were also hundreds of *bachacos*, leaf-cutter ants, walking around the camp. They tear the leaves from trees and carry them to their nest: the load they carry is eight times the weight of their own body. In their nest they let the leaves rot away, and so create the mouldy mass in which they live. One week before the rainy season begins, the queens fly out of the nest, carrying a ball of eggs under their body, to establish new colonies. When they land, they lose their wings. The Pemón try to catch the queens in a net, a risky business, for their bite can be surprisingly vicious; the queens have a nutty flavour, and are so packed with proteins that the Pemón say there is no better way for a man to boost his potency. '*Au moment suprême*, you can knock a grown man off his scooter from the second floor,' Olaf jokingly cited the Dutch comics Koot and Bie. When I seemed sceptical, he just laughed at me: 'Try it sometime; you won't know what to do with yourself.'

We went back to the big hut, only the back wall of which was closed with planks. The front was entirely open; thin strips of wood were nailed to the two sides, with spaces between them big enough to stick your fingers through, so that the wind could always move through. Even in the heat of the day, it remained reasonably cool there. The thatched roof was made of the leaves of the San Pablo palm; it had taken Francisco and Antonio an entire month to weave them together.

Otilia was lying beside her son in the hammock now. The child had stopped coughing. One hour later the boy opened his eyes; his gaze was clearer. By the end of the afternoon the fever had disappeared and he was crawling around the *conuco* again, with an energy that surprised us all.

Francisco had no intention of interfering with our plans, we could do or not do whatever we wanted, as long as we went with him first to see his fields, which were a bit higher than the village, on top of a hill that looked out on the Venado Tepui. Antonio took us up there, the dogs running out in front. Five vultures circled above our heads; when we arrived at the fields, two Amazon parrots flew off, flapping their wings and screeching so loudly that no other bird dared show itself afterwards.

Francisco plucked a soursop from a tree and used his machete to cut open the yellow, melon-sized fruit. Two bites of the sweet-and-sour were enough to quench my thirst. He picked another one as well, for early tomorrow morning.

Antonio inspected the tobacco leaves he had drying on a bamboo grill. He took the biggest leaf, rolled a cigar, lit it, passed it first to me, then to Olaf. The tobacco made my tongue tingle, and reminded me of clove. 'Tastes an awful lot better than one of those things with a filter,' noted Olaf, who had lit his last cigarette on New Year's Eve and was regretting that more and more with each passing day.

Francisco knelt down in the grass and looked through the binoculars Rudy had given him. He was proud of the binoculars, they were the only thing he had kept from the days when he took part in the expeditions Truffino had organized. Within the Indian community, those binoculars must have lent him status; when he returned to the forest in the 1970s, his tribespeople chose him to be their *capitán*. Of course he had the right personality for it as well; after only a few hours, I already regarded him to be one of the most sensible people I had met in the Venezuelan interior. As capitán, he had settled one conflict after another; when the conflicts grew in intensity as alcohol began to flow more freely in the Gran Sabana, he had decided to move further into the jungle with his relatives, and to resign his function. He'd had enough of negotiating with the Venezuelan potentates as well; for the Venezuelans, he said smiling, he had as much respect as for the fleas he scratched off his ass. 'Just like Rudy,' Olaf chimed in. 'He felt like shooting them – literally. Whenever a couple of government inspectors would show up to moan about how he had to start paying taxes on the ground he had claimed, supplemented, of course, with some heavy bribes, Rudy would grab his rifle and fire in the air a few times. And when they turned and ran, he would shout after them: "I am the dictator of Ucaima!"'

Francisco was scanning the steep slopes of the Venado. He couldn't immediately find what he was looking for; after a few minutes, though, his gaze settled on a fixed point, in the deepest part of the jungle, halfway up the mesa.

He handed the binoculars to Olaf.

'Do you see those rocks there in trees? There are petroglyphs painted on them.'

Olaf took off his glasses, adjusted the focus and gave a low whistle.

'Is it possible to get over there?'

'A one-day walk over rough terrain. You have to cut away bushes, and there are boulders under the grass, so you lose your balance every time you take a step.'

That didn't discourage Olaf, though; he had heard about the petroglyphs before, and they served to confirm his idea that other people had lived in the Gran Sabana before the Pemón.

'You want to see them?'

I nodded, not suspecting that I was implictly signing up for the most difficult hike I would ever undertake.

Francisco used the binoculars to follow the flight of a pair of *guacamayas*, blue and red parrots. Then he turned it on Mt. Kurawaina, shimmering vaguely in the distance.

'A hostile tribe came. They chased away the only man who lived at the foot of the mountain. He had the hair of a white man, blond, light, white, and he had a long beard. With the hostile tribe behind him, he fled up the mountain. He climbed to the highest point, then threw himself down. Since then the mountain has been called *Kurawaina*, which means "The man with the white beard." '

He didn't so much tell the story, he sort of sang it. And in the same breath he said: 'It's pretty here. Antonio and I call this point *El Mirador*. We come here every afternoon, just before the sun goes down behind the trees, to look at the mountains.'

With a freight of mangos, yuccas and tobacco leaves, we headed back to the *conuco*. Antonio walked right behind me, and every few steps he shouted: '*Para Jan.*' That meant there was another horsefly on my shirt, ready to draw my blood right through the cotton.

We crossed a little river. I was the last one to reach the far shore, and just as I stepped up onto the riverbank I lost my balance and reached out to steady myself on a rock; at that very moment I felt a sharp pain between my ring finger and my pinky. Was it a wasp? A coral snake? A bushmaster? I'd been looking the other way, and before I even felt the pain penetrating deep into my hand, the culprit had vanished.

Olaf decided it was better to be safe than sorry, and pulled from his pack the little device that looked like a hypodermic needle, except that it ended in a suction cup rather than a needle. He placed the suction cup on the spot where I'd been bitten and pushed down on the plunger: a little knife flicked open, made an incision in the skin, and the suction cup filled with poisoned blood. Back at the *conuco*, he disinfected the wound with alcohol.

It proved effective; the next morning the spot between my fingers was neither red nor swollen. There were, however, two neat little holes on top of my pinky; it must, indeed, have been a snake or a viper.

The incident reminded Olaf of the afternoon he had seen the head of an anaconda sticking out above the rocks in the middle of the creek that winds past the camp at Ucaima. He warned Rudy, who first wanted to check whether the snake had eaten recently. When an anaconda has devoured a small tapir or an agouti, it does not have to feed again for four months, and wouldn't hurt a flea. The problem was to get a look at it: the animal's head resurfaced once every half hour, its huge body remained well hidden under the rocks. Rudy murmured something about his grandchildren playing down here, fetched his revolver, but reconsidered before pulling the trigger – shooting at the head of an anaconda amid the rocks was extremely dangerous; the bullet could ricochet off a stone and come flying back at you at full velocity. In the shed he found a steel pipe; first he drove the pipe into the snake's gullet, then he and Olaf picked up a big rock and dropped it on their end of the pipe. After that, Rudy jammed a big fishhook through the water snake's head and pulled it from under the rocks. As it turned out, the anaconda was dead. He also turned out to have eaten; Rudy cut the snake open and found a young agouti. Then he turned and walked away. He didn't show his face again for the next two days.

The first of the five chickens we had brought with us was bubbling away on the hearthstone; Antonio lit two little votive candles. The sun had barely gone down, and the darkness was already blinding. The only thing we could see coming from the forest were the lantern beetles, which have two little phosphorescent lights dangling above their eyes. Antonio caught one of them, held it close to his face and asked: 'Will I catch a lot of fish tomorrow?' The beetle bit him on the chin, and Antonio said: 'Ah, good. When you bite, I catch a lot.'

The only thing giving the boiled chicken any flavour were the peppers that had been thrown in the pot. Francisco and Antonio were knocking back the cans of beer apace; in the big hut, Florencia and Otilia did the same when their husbands were looking the other way. We had brought enough supplies for five days of quiet drinking, but by the end of the first day our store of Polar had already been almost entirely depleted. Olaf considered it prudent to save the two bottles of rum for another occasion; otherwise the evening would end up in a drunken orgy, and Francisco and Antonio would need days to sleep off their intoxication. Indians are easily overwhelmed by liquor; they lack a certain enzyme in their blood that accelerates the breakdown of alcohol, and therefore stay drunk much longer.

The fire was smouldering; as the evening went on, the monkeys in the forest roared more loudly.

After the next can of beer, Francisco set his hammock a-rocking and began to sing, quietly, melodiously.

'The Song of the Auyán Tepui,' Olaf said.

He translated it for me word-for-word.

'There was once a girl with long, long hair, light was its colour. She had just had her first period, and her mother warned her that she was now susceptible to men. An old sorcerer came by, and she caught his eye. "Be careful," her mother said, "If he gets your attention, he'll put a spell on you, then he'll lure you along and deflower you." The girl went to the darkest part of the hut and kept her eyes fixed on the ground. Then the sorcerer began to sing.'

Francisco dropped his voice an octave.

'I have the sweetest pumpkins, my dearest. I have such sweet pumpkins that the juice runs out of them. Wonderful sweet juice, the finest you'll ever drink.'

Francisco's voice went down another octave.

'That was mean of the sorcerer. He knew how mad she was about pumpkin juice. She jumped up, ran to the opening to the hut and looked at the old sorcerer. The old goat grinned and spoke a magic charm. The first word pulled the girl outside, the second made her fly over the treetops, the third set her down on top of the Auyán Tepui. The sorcerer grabbed the girl with his randy hands, laid her on her back, and her long, light hair fell down. At that spot water began to flow: a long, thin stream that foams white. Since then, every time they come past the waterfall, the Pemón say *Churu Ena*…the girl with the long, light hair.'

The last words he sang about ten times.

Olaf had always been told that the Pemón called the waterfall the '*Churún Meru*'. Francisco saw this as more proof of the white man's total ignorance about the Indians. Pemón is not a uniform language; his tribespeople live in a vast area, far away from each other and separated by almost unscalable mountains; at each settlement, a different form of Pemón is spoken. The people here said '*Churu*', without the 'n'. The Venezuelans heard the Pemón use the word '*meru*' all the time, and claimed that they called Angel Falls the '*Churún Meru*'. But the Pemón use the word '*meru*' to designate a set of rapids or a small waterfall. An '*ena*' is a high waterfall; some of the Pemón said '*vena*', but here they said '*ena*'.

I asked Francisco whether he still saw the Auyán Tepui as a mountain inhabited by demons. He thought long and hard. The only reason why he had climbed the Auyán Tepui a dozen times or more, he said at last, was because Truffino paid the bearers an extra bolívar a day to do it. Of his own free will, he would never have gone wandering around on one of those mesas; they didn't call one of the *tepuis Matawi* for nothing.

And what did *matawi* mean?

'*Quiero morir o suicidio.*'

'In the end,' Olaf said after we had buttoned up the mosquito netting over our hammocks and were lying awake to the ominous shrieks of the howler monkeys, 'Rudy was just as afraid of the Auyán Tepui as the Indians are.'

One evening Rudy and Neil Armstrong were sitting in his lodge close to Angel Falls. From the hole which he had dug at a secret spot in the forest he had taken a bottle of wine, knowing that this always surprised his guests; after a two day journey upriver, there, in the middle of nowhere, they were served a full, red Mendoza or, if the guest was extremely likeable, a vintage Bordeaux. He pulled his oldest Saint-Emilion out of the cellar for the astronaut.

Armstrong, whose weight had almost doubled since the whole world had watched him take his first, cautious steps on the moon, leaned back and said: 'Rudy, I'm going to tell you something not very many people know.'

Right before Apollo 10 began its moon landing, an indefinable object appeared alongside the space capsule, long and tubular as a cigar, dark as a shadow, fairly big. It flew along with the Apollo. All the information about the mysterious object that the astronauts passed along via the radio to ground control, Houston kept out of the live TV broadcast. For security reasons, and probably to prevent all manner of speculation, the information was later erased from the tapes. It was first mentioned in the reports about ten years later, and then only in guarded terms, and more to illustrate the kind of psychological pressure the astronauts were under than as any observation of importance. The object they had seen presented Armstrong with a mystery he found it hard to live with. What exactly was it?

Rudy nodded and listened to the soft hissing of the waterfall.

Then he told Armstrong about the secret he shared with Aleksander Laime.

Laime had fallen once, during the descent of a ravine atop the Auyán Tepui. He hit one boulder after the next, and lost consciousness. He only awoke back at his hut close to Orchid Island. All he could remember was that, during the fall, an animal had grabbed him. An animal with one eye, looking something like a kangaroo, with three toes on each paw.

'And that same animal,' Truffino told Armstrong, 'I once saw too. But I never talk to anyone about it, because they would think I've gone crazy. And maybe I have. You see such mysterious things up there that you actually do feel the madness bearing down on you.'

In my hammock, not far from the huts but at the edge of the *conuco*, almost amid the rustling leaves and snapping twigs of the jungle, it came as no surprise to me to think that Laime and Truffino had started seeing things. But was it only fear muddying their senses? That seemed such an obvious assumption. 'He who lives close to the jungle,' Alejo Carpentier wrote in *Los Pasos Perdidos*, 'lives close to the Unknown.' And the unknown, of course, makes one fearful. But Aleksander Laime and Rudy Truffino had spent almost half their lives in the wilderness; they couldn't have become flustered that easily.

If we can believe Uwe George, who wrote a thoroughly researched article about the Guyanese mesas for *Geo* in March of 1990, three mountain climbers once found the tracks of what must have been a staggeringly large animal atop the Auyán Tepui. The pictures they took of those tracks clearly show the marks of three-toed paws in the dried mud. Paleontologists noted that the only thing comparable to those prints were those of the large reptiles that had once moved on their hind legs.

But Uwe George also took a second possibility into account: that of the existence of a kind of tapir atop the Auyán Tepui that had followed a different evolutionary path, and had little resemblance to the tapirs commonly found elsewhere in the Gran Sabana. That, after all, is exactly what happened with the toads that live on the Auyán Tepui: it's hard to see anything froggish about them. When threatened, they roll themselves up into a ball, and because their backs and legs are completely black, it's almost impossible to distinguish them from the dark rocks. Because of their genetic isolation, the toads, which belong to the family of the *Oreophynella*, look differently on each individual mesa.

Other scientists ridiculed this hypothesis: tapirs cannot climb rock walls. It must have been the thin air and the thick mist, they said, that caused the few who actually found their way up the Auyán Tepui to believe they had seen phantoms. But the rumours continued. In December of 1990, the same magazine, *Geo*, reported that three men in a helicopter had seen a long-necked, saurian creature in a lake on top of the Auyán Tepui. Dr. Armando Michelangeli was one of them. 'Listen,' he told the reporter from *National Geographic* who wanted to know more about this variation on the Loch Ness monster, 'I was there. I saw it. It had a head the size of a rugby ball, and a neck about one foot long. It wasn't an otter, because otters eat fish and there are no fish in that lake. It was not a tapir, because tapirs can't climb cliffs. So what was it? I don't know.'

'Was Laime crazy?' I asked Olaf in the dark.

'He had incredibly bright eyes. When he turned those blue eyes on you, you had the feeling he was looking right through you. One day I went to visit him – I had been to his place with Rudy a few times before that – and he explained to me his theory about the Wei Tepui. That *tepui* consists of two mountains that are entirely symmetrical; the left one the Indians call the Mountain of the Sun, the right one the Mountain of the Moon. Between those two mountains is a gorge, and the sun comes up right in a line with that gorge. Laime figured that that notch was the intersection of the old and the new equators. At the end of the Ice Age, so much ice began to move that the earth was thrown off balance; the equator tilted seven degrees. The point where the old equator and the new equator crossed, Laime said, was precisely in the gorge between those mountains.'

'The lonelier people are, the more creative they become.'

'He didn't just pull that idea out of thin air; he came up with it after he had climbed the Wei. It's an unbelievably difficult climb, the jungle there is more or less impenetrable. In the gorge between the Mountain of the Sun and the Mountain of the Moon, he found the remains of sacrificial temples built thousands of years ago by a people who worked in stone, who worshiped the sun and who had enough knowledge of the universe to build their temples at a spot with a special significance.'

Olaf was silent for a while. The jungle droned on. Then he said: 'So do you understand now why I want to see those petroglyphs?'

The next evening, Francisco told us about the expeditions he had made with Truffino.

We were sitting around the fire on wobbly stools again, eating chicken again, drinking a lot again – rum, this time. The woman walked back and forth until we had finished our meal; then they came and sat with us and asked for a slug from the bottle of Selecto.

Francisco was born in Camarata, the biggest missionary post in the Gran Sabana, about twenty kilometres from the southernmost tip of the Auyán Tepui. In 1957 he had gone north, after hearing that colonists were building a settlement near Canaima. Of the whites he had seen with his own eyes, Truffino was the first who didn't wear a white habit or try to convert him right on the spot.

Before Rudy hired him, he first tested him during a difficult expedition. As it turned out, Francisco was a fast climber who didn't easily lose his good humour, even after a day of heavy carrying, and who understood what Rudy expected from him.

During the second expedition, he kept the other bearers from deserting. Heavy rainfall had slowed down the expedition so much that the supplies ran out. Rudy decided to go back to Canaima, charter a plane and drop new food supplies on top of the Auyán Tepui. When he got back to

Canaima, it turned out that the only plane that touched down at the camp regularly had just left, and Rudy had to wait fifteen days for the next one. During that time, his bearers survived on palm hearts, the only edible thing that grows there atop the mesa. On two separate occasions they had started talking about leaving and getting down off the mountain as quickly as possible, but Francisco convinced them to wait another couple of days. Rudy was grateful to him for that; when he started his new camp at Ucaima, Francisco was one of the only Indians he took with him from Canaima.

Francisco had also worked on the expedition to bring Jimmy Angel's Flamingo down off the mountain, in 1965. He had taken part in the footraces Rudy organized – the starting shot was fired with a real pistol. He had played soccer on the Indian team Rudy had put together. Rudy organized all kinds of activities to keep the Indians from drinking. He was a good person, back then. Then he started earning money, lots of money, and he became a different Rudy. He didn't share the money with the Indians, and Francisco had left. No matter how friendly he was, when it came right down to it he had behaved like a white man, and white men always keep everything for themselves. They are *amunek*, and the Pemón consider that one of the cardinal sins. An exact translation of the word is difficult to give, our 'miserly' or 'greedy' comes closest; there is no real punishment for being *amunek*, the Pemón see it more as a lack of one of the essential values of life, and they avoid the man who thinks only of himself and ignores the interests of the group.

The Pemón had fed Rudy when he was hungry. They had saved his life. Then Rudy became director of the National Park and set the *Guardia Nacional* on them when they shot a tapir. There were already too few wild animals in the forest to start with; the noise of the outboard motors and low-flying planes had chased even those away. And when they finally did succeed in shooting a tapir, the *Guardia* came down on them.

Before Rudy had set up Canaima and Ucaima, there had been only one police post in the region, at Uruyén, on the other side of the Auyán Tepui, a twenty day journey by boat and on foot. The arrival of the *Guardia* was also his doing.

Francisco had moved further east, into areas where no white man ever set foot, but the *Guardia* kept after him. One day four uniformed men were suddenly standing in front of his hut, with a warrant, signed by the director of the National Park: Truffino.

'We were no longer allowed to hunt tapirs, We were no longer allowed to fish with *barbasco*. We were no longer allowed to build new *conucos*.'

In the flickering light of the little candles, I saw Francisco's face grow broader. His voice remained as gentle as ever. The anger went to his jaws, not to his vocal chords.

'We were no longer allowed to live.'

In 1922, the *capítan general* of the Pemón had agreed with the Venezuelan government and the missionaries that the Gran Sabana would become a reservation where the Indians would have a large degree of autonomy, on condition that they abide by the Christian laws and respect the verdicts handed down by the Capuchins in the event of conflicts. For the Indians, it was a matter of choosing the lesser of two evils; in addition to law enforcement, the missionaries would also assume the government's tasks in education; the Church would be granted far-reaching powers, but at the same time it meant that the public authorities would leave the Pemón alone. When gold was discovered on the savannas in the 1930s, the treaty became lost in the shuffle. Then finally the Venezuelan government proclaimed the Gran Sabana a National Park, and the Indians could forget their autonomy.

It was the sons of dictator Pérez Jiménez who had imposed their will on the Venezuelan government; all over the interior, they had held concessions on ground where gold had been found. Francisco had no idea whether Rudy knew about the treaty signed in 1922; by accepting leadership of the National Park, however, he had taken sides with the Venezuelans.

In the highlands, only small patches of ground are actually suitable for farming. The only way the Pemón could survive was by remaining nomads. When they started having to ask permission to build new *conucos*, they saw that not only as a curtailment of their freedom, but also as the beginning of their demise. Most of the Pemón left the jungle, fearing they would die of starvation. They went to work at Canaima, or further away in the cities along the Orinoco. Those who remained behind lived in a constant state of war with the *Guardia Nacional*.

That was how it had happened, and after the last slug of rum Francisco spoke the words with which the Pemón usually finish conversations (or start them).

'*Kaimayek eserumi neke.*'

'I speak no lies.'

'Plenty of hard feelings,' I said in the hammock.

'That's for sure,' Olaf spoke in the darkness. 'They're so shy, the Pemón, so courteous through and through, but when they're in their cups the floodgates are opened.'

'The voice of experience.'

He didn't reply.

'Tell me.'

'My girlfriend. When I lay beside her in the hammock, she wouldn't let me touch her. Cuddling and caressing just wasn't on. She'd push my hands away. She wanted me to go in her, and that was it. That's difficult, man. How do you do that, make love to a woman without taking her in your arms, without touching her back or her hips? I figured she was timid. Until I went with her to a party where they were serving *paracari*, white *cachiri*. The white stuff takes much longer to brew than red *cachiri*, has a lot more alcohol in it, and they only drink it on special occasions. Everyone got plastered, and so did she. And suddenly all the barriers were down. I was no good, I was a white man; she went at me, and then I knew for sure.'

'What?'

'Tenderness doesn't exist in the jungle.'

What the Pemón didn't understand, Olaf said, was that Rudy had gradually begun to get a clearer picture of the dangers facing the highlands. Every time the Indians built a new *conuco*, they burned down a bit of forest to prepare the soil and to attract game – the new grass that grows among the ashes draws deer and tapirs. The number of forest fires had grown to around ten thousand a year, which is why the Venezuelans had given *los Pemónes* the nickname los *Quemones*, 'the arsonists'.

During his first years in the Gran Sabana, Rudy had been just as excited about hunting tapir as the Indians were. When a full-grown tapir feels cornered, it comes thundering at you through the brush with its full two hundred kilos. The Indians regarded the tapir hunt as a trial by fire; a man is only a man once he has brought down a tapir. Rudy didn't see it all too differently; if there was anyone who needed to prove himself each and every day anew, it was Rudy. But the number of tapirs quickly dwindled, and in the early 1970s, as director of the National Park, he had no choice but to declare the tapir an endangered species. If he hadn't, there wouldn't be a single tapir walking around amid the mesas today.

When Rudy found a young tapir in the woods, he would take it back to the camp so it could regain its strength. What usually happened then was that the Indians chased the fattened animal into the savanna, then roasted it on a spit the next day. Rudy tried to explain to them that they were compromising their own future; the Pemón would nod knowingly, but had no idea what he was talking about. Their language has no words for next week or next month. Today and tomorrow are the only designations for time.

At the end of his life, Rudy would jump back and forth across a forest path in order not to step on ants. He had stopped hunting long before that; he only took his rifle with him to ward off danger in an emergency. He may have lived far from the civilized world, but like most Westerners he had awakened to the destructive power of mankind. Every intervention in nature disturbed the balance; the further the Indians moved into the forest, the more damage they caused; after the fires came the erosion, turning the vast forests into barren flats. Francisco might accuse him of meddlesomeness, but the Pemón were unable to see past their own *conuco*, while Rudy had been responsible for the entire Gran Sabana – a biological goldmine just screaming to be protected.

Of course there were more things Francisco resented about his former employer: his stinginess, his egoism, his *amunek*. According to Olaf, Rudy didn't earn much on the expeditions. Even later, when Ucaima became popular, he didn't live high on the hog. Every potato served at the camp had to be flown in, and that cost a pretty penny. Once the guests had left, Rudy and Gerti went back to eating canned sardines; with three daughters attending the expensive Von Humboldt boarding school, there was no money for meat.

In the 1970s, Rudy renovated the camp. He bought a water pump, a second generator, a Landrover, a plane. He was a lousy pilot, he had flipped his Cessna on three separate occasions while making a sloppy landing. The insurance paid for only part of the damage; nevertheless, after each crash he bought a new plane. How he was able to pay for it all is a secret he took with him to his grave.

There were two common rumours. One said that he was somehow involved in drug smuggling. The big cocaine plantations are just across the Colombian border from the Gran Sabana, and Venezuela is known as a transit country. Olaf didn't completely rule out that possibility, but he had known Rudy well enough to know that, as director of the National Park, he wouldn't have risked his official function by maintaining dealings with criminals or people with criminal connections. What's more, he had never made any arrangements with the Venezuelan government about the piece of land he had claimed in Ucaima. He was balancing on the verge of the possible and the permitted, and he was smart enough not to give the Venezuelans a reason to send him packing.

Olaf considered it more likely that he had found gold or gems. The huge amount of documentation I had found in his archives about the finds at San Salvador de Paul in the early 1970s point in that same direction. According to an interview he gave to *The New York Times*, he must have been among the first to dig at San Salvador. The news that amazing strikes had been made close to that town spread across the country like wildfire. Hundreds of adventurers moved to the savannas south of Canaima, bus drivers from Carácas, waiters, cattle farmers from the llanos and an army of the unemployed – twelve to fifteen planes a day arrived at Canaima. But Rudy had been there before them.

The first thing one saw in San Salvador, he told the American journalist, was a military camp with four or five tents, and enormous tarps hanging in front of them to catch rainwater. There was no drinking water; the Río Caroni was at least an hour's walk. The town consisted of hastily built shops to sell tools to the diamond hunters; cafeterias, bars, pool halls, a bingo hall and a brothel. The latter two were the busiest places in town. You never saw policemen; they were out digging for themselves, out panning in the savanna, shoulder to shoulder with hundreds of other poor bastards. No one there paid attention to what anyone else did, it was every man for himself and malaria for all.

Later he told Olaf that he had stayed there for weeks, and that he had been very ill when he came back. But he probably also brought back some gems that solved his financial problems.

The camp had just been thoroughly renovated when Camel decided to start shooting its commercials in the Gran Sabana. The film crew landed at Ucaima twice a year. Rudy didn't ask much for scientific expeditions, but he let the tobacco company pay and pay.

And so he swung from one extreme to the other, a fat wallet one day, broke the next.

He wasn't stingy, but Gerti was. After she died, he hired seven or eight Indians; Pemóns always accompanied him on his trips. He paid them well, but he also saw what the Indians did with their money: they bought beer and rum. The more he gave them, the more frequently they stayed away to sleep off their drunkeness or to hang around a little longer in Canaima, close to the girls. In the long run they became as

Venezuelan as the Venezuelans; every hangover had to be rinsed away in more alcohol, and preferably in the company of the fairer sex.

Venezuelans amuse themselves, always. That their country is plagued by natural disasters and uprisings, military coups and acts of violence, inflation and corruption, is something they never let get in the way of a good time. As far as they're concerned, the wilder the better; every Venezuelan, at least once in his life, performs an absolutely rash deed. Their sense of logic may abandon them often enough, their fantasy never does. They are, however, an impossible people to work with. Appointments are forgotten as soon as they are made, contracts are lost almost before they're signed; negligence is the rule, impropriety law. At first Rudy forgave the Venezuelans a great deal, because they had so generously accepted him in their midst, but after a while he tired of the eternal wheeling and dealing, and spoke of his new compatriots as lazy, raunchy and unreliable.

And he was deeply disappointed to see the Pemón assuming all their worst characteristics. True, he was the one who had put them in contact with the Western way of living, but he couldn't understand why they no longer trusted their shamans, why they suddenly came to see their influence as dangerous, why they threw overboard everything in which they had believed for generations. He travelled to meet the Yanomami, he read about other Indian peoples, only to conclude at last that the Pemón were too meek. Their loveliest side was also their weakest: they were too receptive to outside influences. Like the Venezuelans, they had begun eating huge quantities of meat. They switched from the vitamin-rich *cachiri* to beer, and so lost their athletic prowess. They turned to the prophets of the Hallelujah Movement or the San Miguel

Movement or other Adventist sects, whose evangelists had blown in from British Guiana like a swarm of parasitic flies.

David John Thomas discovered precisely how pernicious that new influence was when he studied the Pemón way of life. The prophets of the Hallelujah Movement mixed all kinds of Christian elements with old Indian rituals, and interpreted the journey which the shaman's soul makes to heaven as an attempt to come in contact with the God of the Christians. They danced the Indians' dances, sang the melodies of their songs, but the lyrics cast suspicion on the shamans and praised the Redeemer as the indisputable saviour in times of need, which only confused the Pemón further. The Capuchins had already drastically changed the way they lived; the prophets threw them into a deep spiritual crisis, which ended with them turning their backs on their shamans.

Culture is like a building; saw away a few supporting beams, and the whole thing comes tumbling down. The Capuchins had knocked over the first pillars of Indian culture in the Gran Sabana; the Adventists, civil servants and thrill-seekers did the rest. They convinced the Pemón of their good intentions – and before the Indians fully realized who they were dealing with, they had no roof over their heads. For, no matter how incomprehensible it may have been to most white people, their belief in the shamans had protected them for centuries against all evils.

Rudy grew bitter. He resigned as director of the National Park. It had never been much more than a paper function anyway; he lacked the ways and means to truly protect the Gran Sabana, and he had no desire to act as a buffer between the Venezuelan government and the Indians any longer. He had the growing sense that he was standing at the end of an era, and for someone who had been used to pioneering all his life, that was a hard thing to accept. No, he hadn't brought the Indians good fortune, only trouble, and he knew that the elders blamed him for that, men like Francisco, men he respected because they had remained true to the Indian traditions, and with whom he actually had much more in common than with city people who couldn't tell a toucan from a macaw.

'But it's easy enough for Francisco to be critical,' Olaf said. 'How much rum is left in that bottle?'

'Not a drop.'

'I have a little backup supply, I'll surprise him with that tomorrow.'

'And so we assist them in their demise.'

'Oh yeah, I've heard that before. But could you imagine the look on Francisco's face if we hadn't pulled the Selecto out of our packs? Those eyes of his aren't watery from old age, he needed a drink. And what was the last thing he said to Florencia tonight? That she should spit in the *cachiri*. That makes it ferment faster. Gives it more alcohol.'

It was a shaman who showed Rudy the best place to build his camp. According to Francisco, Ramón Figiroa had influenced Rudy a great deal. He advised him to build an Indian settlement close to the camp at Ucaima; life in the jungle would be sure to confront him with new problems on a daily basis, and with an Indian community close by he could always go to ask for help and advice. So just south of Ucaima, Rudy cleared a plot of land and he and Francisco built four huts on it, which the Montes moved into. Francisco continued to live there for years, until all the soil around the *conuco* had been depleted. 'He came by every day,' Francisco recalled, 'and never made a decision without talking to me about it first.'

That was wise of him, I said to Francisco, and he reluctantly agreed. But then he started in about the tapirs again, and asked me, while he looked me straight in the eye: 'Have you ever really been hungry?'

That night a steady rain of leaves fell on my mosquito net. By first light I saw that the net was crawling with ants. The tree above my hammock was bare; in one night the cutter ants had divested it of all its foliage. Beneath my hammock I saw the ants walking off by the hundreds, in squads of two, with leaves on their backs many times their own size.

I climbed out of the hammock and wiped the tears from my eyes. The whole night I had been lying in the smoke of the smoldering fire meant to keep the snakes at bay, and the jaguar that had its eye on the dogs. Just before sun-up Florencia had tossed more wood on it. There was a fire going in the big hut as well, and the entire *conuco* was filled with smoke. My hair smelled of charcoal, so did my clothes, and I coughed so loudly that it woke Olaf.

The dogs went with me when I retired to the bushes; they sniffed at my hole when I dropped my pants. A horsefly latched onto my one buttock, and a pair of ticks moved in for breakfast on the other. Taking a dump in the jungle was no easy business. Olaf was apparently finding it equally arduous; from behind the bushes, I heard him yelling, 'Holy shit!' at the dogs.

Francisco waddled over to his hammock in the compound and ate the remains of the chicken and rice from the evening before; Florencia asked whether I'd like some too. Meat on an empty stomach seemed too much for me at the start of the day; I cast a glance at the soursop, and Florencia cut it open for me right away. 'Now you know why I've never taken another wife,' Francisco said. 'I could have had two or three, our people allow polygamy, but she was so nice that I never looked at another woman again.' A child cried, she picked it up and lifted it into the sling around her neck. That was how it went all day long; every childish wail was immediately stifled, and sometimes Florencia and Otilia carried two children on their shoulders at once.

As I washed in the river, the minnows darted between my legs. Antonio was standing a little further along the bank. He giggled. I didn't understand why; maybe he wasn't completely sober yet. He went back to his hammock, petted his cuddly beast, and fell asleep again. It reminded Olaf of the mouse he had once carried with him everywhere in a fold of his T-shirt, back when he was fifteen and at odds with the world. He had even slept with that mouse. One night, though, he rolled over on top of it; when he woke up in the morning, the mouse had suffocated.

Francisco used his machete to scrape the green bark off the stems of the *manare* and cut it into strips. His bowed legs could hardly carry him anymore, but his fingers were still as supple as elastic. He used the strips to weave a basket. Occasionally he cast a glance at my shoes. 'Nice shoes.' 'More or less my size.' 'Did you bring another pair with you?' His shoes had no laces, and were worn at the heels.

Olaf lit the cigar Antonio had rolled for him, and sat down on a stool. It was ten in the morning, and he was starting on his first bowl of *cachiri*, in the hope that the yucca fibers would activate his intestines.

After a couple of sips he started talking about his mentor again. Rudy had made an incredible impression on him, but he could still never really impose any order on his recollections. Maybe, as he never tired of saying, it was because

222

he had never met anyone who so clearly combined both the good and the bad. The good memories sometimes obscured the bad ones, and vice versa.

'After all,' he said in Spanish then, 'he was bad news, too.'

Francisco nodded; I closed the little book in which I had been taking notes.

'One time, in Carácas, he was robbed in the street. One of those little criminals pushed him up against the wall, frisked him, took the revolver out of his belt and the wallet out of his inside pocket, and walked away. Rudy knew what was going to happen: before he got to the corner, the boy would turn and shoot him down. In Venezuela, robbery will get you thirty years in prison; Rudy had seen the guy up close, and could give a good description of him. That's why muggers in Carácas would rather play it safe. But Rudy had learned from the Pemón that you should always carry two weapons; if one of them jams, you've always got the other one. Rudy leaned down, pulled the second pistol out of his boot, and shot the kid dead. He hurried back to his apartment, shaved off his beard, hopped on the plane and laid low in the Gran Sabana for a month.'

Francisco's watery eyes twinkled.

'They were all a little trigger-happy. Jerry Bunt, Anyatoli, Rudy. When they saw a Venezuelan coming in the distance, they started shooting. We loved that: a Venezuelan never came to deliver good news. Anyatoli would even shoot at the *Guardia Nacional*. Ha, but he was always drunk. They were all pretty crazy, completely nuts in fact, but not afraid. 'When the tiger is in the man,' we say around here, 'the man becomes a tiger.'

Then his gaze moved to my feet again.

'Sturdy shoes, Jan. Heavy soles. Those will last a long time.'

The next day they would indeed prove their worth, when the fire took us by surprise.

By first light I saw an Indian sitting on a stool beside my hammock, with last night's bounty across his knees, a rodent he had draped across his tattered trousers like a fur. At his feet lay a rusty rifle, a breechloader that could fire only one shot.

I pushed aside the mosquito netting and nodded to the Indian. He looked at me searchingly, with big, serious, patient eyes, as though he couldn't quite believe that he was seeing a blonde head come out from under the netting. The jump from the hammock to my shoes was fast, but before I had even tied the laces the first louse had nestled in my sock. My day started with an itch.

The Indian waved away the flies that were drawn in bunches to the blood dripping from the mouth of the *lapa*.

'Here, feel,' he said.

He grabbed my wrist and pressed my hand against the capybara's swollen stomach.

'Enough meat for days.'

The *lapa* was about one metre long, and must have weighed thirty kilos.

'Too much for one man.'

So, in order to provide a few of his tribesmen with a hefty meal, he had come walking to Francisco's *conuco*.

His own *conuco* was a little further along, on the other side of the hill. He lived there alone, at least for the time being.

That was undoubtedly the most important fact of all to him, and after he had told me that he gave me his name.

'Victorino Manrique.'

His face was broad, like Francisco's. I saw no sense in asking whether they were related; all that would follow would be a Babel-like confusion of terms. It was only the night before that I had finally realized that Antonio was not Francisco's son, but his son-in-law; Francisco referred to him, however, as 'my son'. In Pemón, that word also has a double meaning: it can refer to both 'son' and 'sperm'. At least, that is, when a man is talking about his son; a woman uses two different words, '*me*' or '*rume*', but both of those may also refer to her daughter. Francisco also called Antonio 'my brother', because the Pemón recognize two ways of being someone's brother: by having the same father, or by sharing certain experiences. It was more complicated than algebra, and without help from Thomas it would have remained a long equation of misunderstandings to me. The dog-eared photocopies from his book, however, provided clarity: among the Pemón, the man moves in with his wife's parents, and the ties with his in-laws are the strongest of all.

Before Victorino gave the *lapa* to Florencia, he petted the animal's head one last time. Florencia had already poked up the fire and put a pan of water on the hearthstones. I never ceased to be amazed at her industriousness; despite her age, she was the most active person at the *conuco*. As the water boiled, she held the capybara above the pan by its hind legs. The steam loosened the skin, and a little later she could begin skinning the *lapa* with a machete. Her grandchildren watched; Antonio and Olaf had now risen from their hammocks.

'It's been months since I saw a *lapa*,' Antonio sighed.

Victorino turned a critical eye on him, then said with

inexorable logic: 'Follow the tracks.'

'But I haven't seen *lapa* tracks for months.'

Then Victorino affected modesty.

'I only saw them by chance.'

Antonio could live with that explanation. He bared his teeth, laughed too loudly, slapped Victorino on the shoulder and said: 'Victorino knows this area better than anyone. He can show us the way to the petroglyphs.'

Olaf was immediately wide awake. Was it half a day's walk, or would it take a full day, he asked. Victorino figured that, if we hurried, we could be back before sundown. 'But then we should actually get going,' Olaf suggested. Victorino shouldered his rifle; as far as he was concerned, we could leave right now. He hadn't slept all night, but walking is one thing to which the Pemón have no aversion. Antonio went to the big hut to look for his boots. Francisco, visibly irritated at having to stay behind with the women, took me aside.

'All well and good,' he said, 'but this is one trip you don't write about.'

He had to repeat it for me a few times; I could barely imagine that an old man who had never held a book, a newspaper or a magazine would be worried about what I might put on paper.

'It's the *Guardia Nacional*. You're going to climb a *tepui*. That's not allowed. You have to ask permission first, in Canaima. That takes a lot of time and a lot of money. If they find out that you went up there with our help, we'll be in trouble. They'll come here to the *conuco* and they won't go away until they've eaten and drunken everything they can find. The last time they bothered Otilia. Grabbing her breasts and things. They think they can get away with anything.'

He spat on the ground.

'You can't write about the gold either.'

'Gold?'

'You're going to cross a savanna full of gold. No one must know exactly where that is.'

Francisco talked about gold all the time. About golden ducats in the river, about gold nuggets supposedly lying under the sand of the savanna, about flakes of gold other tribesmen had seen glistening in a stream. While at Francisco's *conuco*, I came to see a new nuance in the El Dorado legend: who had actually whetted whose gold lust? I promised Francisco I would be vague about the route we took. Then he warned us to keep the dogs close to us: last night he had heard the tiger wail.

Feeling reassured, we set out on our journey.

The first stretch followed a reasonable path through low woods. We had to cross a river, which soaked us to the waist right away, and then climb a hill, but just about the time I started feeling my calf muscles, we started on the descent along a path made slippery by a layer of dead leaves. Antonio slid, landed hard, and blamed his boots. He, too, was beginning to show interest in my shoes.

Two hours later we reached Victorino's *conuco*, two newly built huts in an opening cleared by fire. We had to stop and admire the *waipa*, the big hut, which did not have the classic oval shape but was long and high as a hangar, and the little hut in which he had built an oven with stones from the river so he could bake his own manioc cakes, and the table between the huts, sturdy and made from pieces of bamboo lashed together with roots, and the cotton plants that were blossoming now and from which he hoped to pick the cotton in a few days' time. He poured us a bowl of *cachiri*, fetched us a bunch of bananas and a few overripe mangos, and pointed out the place where his wife and the two children would sleep: the preparations had been made, and soon they would arrive here, along with his father-in-law. He nodded contentedly.

Balancing on a fallen trunk, we crossed the river from which Victorino took most of his food; he sometimes ate only fish for weeks on end. We walked through thick jungle for the next hour. When we arrived at the savanna, the impression was that of stepping out of the night into the day. The yellow of the grass blinded us, the orange of the bromeliads flared. Antonio pointed out deer and tapir tracks in the sand, Victorino led us past the collapsed entrance to a mine once dug by an American, George LeRoy, originally a rancher from Oklahoma who had hoped to strike it rich here. In the late 1950s he had landed at Canaima, in the 1960s he began to dig on the savanna. He found nothing. Since then he had been cleaning toilets at the camp in Canaima, or begging in the yard in front of the souvenir shop, at least when he wasn't locked up in the jail at Cíudad Bolívar. With every cent he earned, he bought liquor, and once fortified with rum he would knock out the teeth of some random passer-by. Not every adventurer made good in the wilds; George LeRoy became a wreck.

The tall grass whipped against our hands, the sun stung, the dogs were driven mad by the grasshoppers. Otherwise the crossing went without incident.

The hike became truly difficult when we started the climb to the rocks with the petroglyphs on them, halfway up the steep wall of the Venado Tepui. Victorino and Antonio's machetes swung constantly, hacking away branches and vines that blocked our path. Sometimes we became hopelessly stuck in the undergrowth, and had to go back to find another hole in the wall of green. At the same time, every step was a misstep, the grass hid the exact shapes of rocks and stones, and we often sank up to our ankles in a crevice and had to pull our shoes out by force. The breath of wind that had first been coming from the northeast was gone entirely now; we were climbing the mountain from the south, and the south face was steaming in the sun. Antonio and Victorino didn't seem bothered by the heat, but because Indians eat so little salt they barely sweat; my body, however, was pouring out litres of it. In addition to the heat, I also struggled against the itch. Every time I went crawling through the brush, ticks would jump me from all sides; they had no trouble finding the gaps in my clothing, and clamped on to my arms and legs. I had also brought a few sand fleas with me from the savanna.

After the first ridge came a section that was a little less steep. Ferns grew there, rather than bushes, and the trees were enormous. There were dozens of orchids hanging from every trunk, most of them in bloom: red, orange and, above all, purple.

'Rudy,' Olaf said, 'once talked about an area on the other side of a savanna where he collected orchids. He was pretty secretive about it, he only took experts along with him. That must have been here.'

We climbed again, and became hopelessly tangled in a snarl of branches, vines and roots. Back. Victorino said he knew another route, along a dry streambed, but thorny bushes had sprung up there now and tore at our clothes, and soon at our arms and legs as well. Back again. The third attempt was successful. While cutting a path, Victorino and Antonio slashed a hornets' nest in two and had to dive off into a ditch, their hands held in front of their faces. They wailed as though they were being beaten; Indians are more afraid of hornets than of jaguars or black panthers, and will turn and run as soon as they see a nest. Victorino and Antonio crept along as though the devil was after them – but, during their escape, they found a way through.

'Shit, man,' Olaf said, 'no living person has ever come this way.'

'Oh yes they have, otherwise there wouldn't be any petroglyphs.'

'But it makes you wonder which path the first inhabitants took on their way up here.'

'Victorino must have been here before, right?'

'I think he's just following his hunches. We're going downhill more than we're climbing.'

The zigzagging came to an end when Victorino set course for the far left side of the south face. The terrain there was passable, although one time he did have to throw his full weight against the vegetation in order to open a hole in what looked to be an impenetrable hedge.

'Old Samson had nothing on him,' Olaf said, and clapped loudly.

The transition was abrupt, as all transitions are in the Gran Sabana. After the last climb we suddenly found ourselves on a broad path that ran along a rock wall thirty metres high. Had this once been built as a road? Or was it simply that nothing would grow in this gravelly soil?

The petroglyphs were painted in red pigment on a smooth piece of basalt. Dashes with circles around them, spirals, little stick figures that looked more like a symbol than like any attempt to depict human beings, a thing with a lizard's head and a fish's tail. The petroglyphs showed no refinement, they were more like the chalk drawings children make on a playground, the hatchmarks they make to keep score in some game they're playing.

Every traveller through the area between the Orinoco and the Amazon has come across these figures; first Von

Humboldt and Bonpland, then Wallace, Spruce, Koch-Grünberg, Gheerbrant, Carpentier, and more recently, Redmond O'Hanlon. The marks O'Hanlon saw close to the Rio Negro, a good four hundred kilometres south of here, exhibited so many similarities to these that they must have been painted by the same people. 'Matchstick men with multiple arms or box bodies, abstract designs of whorls and circles and lines, crude representations of iguanas or fish.' Spruce believed that the symbols were drawn by the ancestors of the Indians, and that their level of civilization was no higher – and probably lower – than their modern-day descendants. But Spruce also saw in them the first, cautious attempts at art, while the petroglyphs were sooner some kind of indicators – 'of where the gold is to be found,' Francisco had said to us a few days earlier. Or, what seemed more likely to me, as route directions for fellow tribesmen.

Olaf had no doubt that there was a link between the petroglyphs, the crypts and the sun temple about which Laime had told him in that rare candid moment. He photographed the symbols down to the smallest detail.

'I want to use these photos to get a few archaeologists interested in going along with me. Experts in pre-Columbian cultures. A real expedition, like the ones Rudy organized in the fifties and sixties. That would be fantastic. Searching. An enormous kick. Making links. Finding what's been hidden for a long time. Discovering.'

Victorino and Antonio said there was no way a Pemón could have painted these symbols.

'We don't even use red paint!'

The Pemón didn't draw or make tattoos either.

'These stick figures don't mean anything to us.'

So who *had* painted them?

They shrugged.

'*Pena.*'

Everything earlier than yesterday the Pemón refer to as '*pena*' – 'times gone by', and for them bygone times remain as unfathomable as the distant future. When they say '*pena*', the Pemón mean that they know nothing about it; the past never reveals its secrets.

'Maybe there are more in there,' Victorino said, pointing to a cleft in the rock.

We entered the shadowy cave, the dogs out in front. After about twenty metres they froze, whining; at the same moment Antonio pushed Olaf aside and jumped forward.

Antonio possessed a sixth sense. He wasn't nearly as strong as Victorino, he was skinny and short, but he was prepared. Before we had gone into the cave he had picked up a sturdy branch, and now he was whipping the ground with it. '*Djjang, djjang,*' he grunted, pressing the air out between his lips, and with a final hiss the bushmaster gave up the ghost. The adder was at least a metre and half long.

'Where there's one, there are bound to be more,' Victorino predicted. Moist as the cave was, with all the cracks and crevices between the rocks, it must indeed have been an ideal spot for snakes. Because we had no lanterns with us, we decided to return to daylight.

Before the rock wall, Antonio and Victorino tied two hammocks to the trees. The trip back would be twice as hard, they said, so Olaf and I should rest a little. Meanwhile they would go down the hill a hundred metres or so, to a streambed there, and roast a chicken. They disappeared into the bushes, and minutes later we could still hear Antonio speaking excitedly in a high voice. Victorino may have killed a *lapa*, but he had been too fast for a bushmaster; he had proven his worth, and that counted in a place where every step could be your last.

Smoke came curling up, the smell of roasted meat floated our way. Antonio came to get us. We folded up the hammocks and followed him. Victorino was squatting by the fire alongside a river that must have been a raging torrent in the rainy season, and now, after months of drought, still babbled away like a brook. Antonio brought us our appetizer; a yellowish-brown ribbon which he picked up off a rock at the end of a stick and held before our eyes, so we could see the head from close by, its forked tongue dangling. Once again, a bushmaster, this one two metres long, and once again clubbed to death by Antonio. He burst into uncontrollable laughter.

Olaf pulled a jar out of his pack and sprinkled herbs on the chicken. Wherever he went, he always took a mixture of basil, parsley and fennel with him, and a bottle of Tabasco sauce. This latter addition pleased Victorino and Antonio greatly; to them, meat only tasted good when it burned in your mouth. We drank water from the stream and finished the meal with the bananas we'd taken with us from Victorino's *conuco*.

The sun was at least two hours past its zenith when we started back. Victorino led the way, and he kept up a chilling pace. I felt the blood pounding in my temples, and soon it was knocking away above my eyebrows as well. My legs and feet wanted to move along, but the hammers in my head warned me that I was steadily approaching my limit. An invisible hand tried to squeeze my pupils closed, and I could only focus by stopping for a moment. I fell dozens of metres behind; the only one who seemed worried about that was the smallest of the two dogs, the white one the Indians called *Copita*, 'snowflake'. Whenever the others would disappear into the brush or jump down over a ledge, Copita would stand there waiting for me, and would move on again only when I had approached to within a metre. 'If you only knew,' I said half out loud, 'how much I detest dogs,' but he seemed oblivious to my cynicism, and paid just as little heed to the barking of the other dog, who was losing his patience with our loitering.

The final few hundred metres downhill, Victorino jumped from rock to rock; there was no keeping up with him, a strange fever was driving him to a murderous pace, and at last it was Antonio who asked him to slow down a bit. Still, he crossed the savanna at a trot. When he got to the next stretch of jungle and smelled the odor of burning wood, he raced out ahead.

His *conuco* had burned down. One hour later we stood before the smoking remains of his huts. He walked around amid it all, his arms held out wide, more helpless than panicky; he stopped in front of a charred rafter, and kicked at another; he bent over a piece of bent steel and saw that it was the serrated edge of his saw. All that was left of his clothing was a pile of ashes, the leather of his spare shoes was blackened. The cotton plants had been devoured by the flames as well, as had the mango trees, the bananas and the manioc.

There was no way to tell how the fire had started; the night before, Victorino had burned away some weeds, and perhaps the fire in the grass had continued to smolder. Or maybe he hadn't completely put out the fire in the oven. Or – and Antonio took this possibility into serious account – a tribesman had taken advantage of Victorino's absence to get revenge on him. Victorino wanted to check on this latter possibility right away; he walked down the path to the river and returned a little later, shaking his head. He had found no footprints anywhere, except for ours.

The flames had leapt to the forest, and a large part of the valley was now burning as well. In order not to be cut off by the fire, Victorino recommended that we move on quickly.

'What about you?' Olaf asked.

'Later. Later.'

He wasn't upset, at least not visibly; he controlled himself admirably, but refused to put up with any objections.

'Shall we go?' Antonio asked.

The dogs barked, jumped up against each other, ran in little circles; the fire was driving them mad with fear.

We walked on; Antonio coughing incessantly, Olaf sniffing, me wiping the tears from my eyes. The smoke hurt my throat, and I pressed a handkerchief over my mouth and nostrils. The burning trees crackled and boomed dully, the flames leapt up metres all around us.

'Jesus,' Olaf hissed, 'I hope we make it out of here alive.'

Antonio started running, and we followed at a trot. The fire had spread out along the edge of the valley. We were surrounded on all sides, and had no choice but to jump right through the burning brush. Antonio was the first to plunge into the fire, Olaf followed, the biggest of the two dogs right behind him. I was just about to make my leap when I saw Copita standing there, paralyzed with fear, his mouth wide open. He was afraid to jump. I hesitated; he gave a little yelp, something that sounded like the noise a baby makes sometimes after being fed. Olaf must have heard it, for suddenly he was right in front of me. He grabbed the dog, held him to his chest and made another dash for it. People like that, I thought, are right for the jungle; bold, quick-minded, however critical they may be of themselves – Olaf complained repeatedly that he couldn't concentrate for more than two minutes at a time.

Except for smoke and the occasional flame, I could see nothing. I felt branches hitting my shins and, if I wasn't mistaken, I felt the fire licking at one of my trouser legs; my feet swelled from the heat, my shoes pinched, but the soles did not melt. The next thing I saw was Olaf's backpack; he squatted down, put the dog back on the ground and said: 'At least we got out of there.' Copita immediately began licking his hand.

We climbed the hill; the fire was now behind us. The higher we came, the more clearly we could see the extent of the blaze: a broad, pinkish river, meandering ten or fifteen kilometres through the forest.

Antonio was waiting at the top, in the company of four Indians who had seen the column of smoke on the horizon and left right away to see whether Victorino needed help. Antonio stood talking to them for a long time. We grew impatient, darkness was falling and we still had a good hour to go.

'You two go on.'

'All right,' Olaf said.

At the bottom of the hill we came to a fork in the path, and hesitated about whether to take the narrow way or the broader one.

'It must be that one,' Olaf said, pointing at the broader one.

After half an hour – or had forty-five minutes gone by already? – we realized that the smoke was getting closer. We were approaching the fire again, and had circled back around to the valley from which we had just fled.

'I figured that was it,' Olaf said in an irritatingly lighthearted tone. 'It was the other path; this morning we took the narrow one.'

We returned to the fork.

The last bit of light had left the sky, the forest was assuming phantom shapes on both sides of the path.

'Look, look!' Olaf shouted.

I saw something go shooting by.

Hounded by the fire, the wild animals were running for safety. And any animal, even the smallest, can become aggressive when panicked.

'I hope it was a giant anteater,' Olaf said. 'I've always wanted to see one of those. *Oso palmera* the Venezuelans call them; their tail is shaped like a palm leaf.'

'Oh sure, keep acting tough.' I was swaying on my feet. 'Except for that dull machete of yours, we don't have anything with us. No rifle, nothing. We should never have left without Antonio. They know this area. You only think you know it!'

He smiled serenely.

'Half an hour from now you'll be lying in your hammock, eating *lapa*. Wanna bet?'

'Let's hope so.'

His smile froze. What I saw in his eyes then looked an awful lot like pity.

'You're finished, man. You've had it. Your face is as red as a beet.'

The next moment I heard myself screaming in a rage I had never known was in me. I had read about it in the accounts; in the deepest of the jungle, fear and fatigue bring out the worst in a man. But when you read things like that in the comfort of your den, you're always convinced that you yourself would stay cool under identical circumstances. I cursed my travelling companion black and blue. It speaks well of him to say that he turned around calmly and walked away, as though I'd had to vomit and he preferred not to watch.

The dogs got up, their tongues hanging halfway to the ground as well.

We took the narrow path, waded through a stream in utter darkness, stumbling over submerged stones. In long, dark wails, a howler monkey bellowed his outrage through the jungle, owls flew off in fright, crickets chirped louder than in the heat of the day, frogs and toads sounded their alarm. Everything that lived had gone mad with tension.

Then we heard a familiar shuffling.

Holding a lantern in front of his bare stomach, Francisco came waddling up to us.

'Over here,' he waved to us, in one and the same movement swatting away the mosquitos that were drawn by the dozen to the light and latching onto his shoulders.

He pursed his lips and produced two notes that echoed through the jungle for minutes. As they slowly died away, an equally melodious reply came from the far distance. Antonio had gone looking for us as well.

'Stay close to me,' Francisco panted. He coughed up a laugh that rattled around in his throat. 'I told Antonio; when you go out with a white man you always have to hold onto him by the seat of the pants, otherwise you'll lose him in the forest.'

Florencia was cutting strips of meat off the *lapa* while Otilia dished piles of rice onto the plates. When Victorino came into the camp, they went on imperturbably. They didn't look at him, they didn't nod to him, they concentrated on what they were doing. Victorino brushed the ashes out of his hair, came and took a stool, drank two cups of *cachiri* back to back and sank his teeth into the meat.

'Good meat,' he said. 'Juicy. Tender.'

It had been boiled, and no matter how I chewed on it, I couldn't taste much at all. Olaf sprinkled his chunk with Tabasco; Victorino went on growling in approval; tapir was better, of course, but he had eaten tougher *lapa*s. Egged on by Florencia and Otilia, Antonio listed all the birds he liked to eat, and after each name he made a clicking noise with his tongue. Francisco sang a song about hunting a tiger, pulled old Florencia to her feet, danced a few steps with her and blared: 'You're just like my sweetheart, my tiger, I'll have you soon enough.'

Olaf tried to steer the conversation towards the fire. Victorino squinted at him, as though he were trying to pick a fight. What were his plans now, Olaf inquired. Victorino shrugged and went on eating.

I offered him my hammock; we would be leaving in a day or two, and there was no reason why he shouldn't keep my hammock. It sank in only slowly... hammock, hammock... good, hammock.

'And your shoes,' Francisco added quickly.

'Listen, Francisco, I can't walk back in my bare feet.'

'You can't?'

He was genuinely surprised.

'That's too bad.'

Then he held up his plate; he was ready for another slab of *lapa*.

The next day began with cries of pain from behind the bushes. The barking dogs at my side, I went to look. We found Olaf squatting there, a pair of tweezers and a wad of cotton in his hands. He had his pants down around his knees; at his feet was a bottle of alcohol.

'Ticks,' he shouted to me from afar. 'In the worst possible place a man can have them.'

'Hmm, I'm afraid you'll have to take care of that one yourself.'

His reply consisted of a curse, and a long, drawn-out shriek.

Carrying a bar of antibacterial soap and clean clothes, we went down to the stream. Olaf walked as though he'd just been castrated.

'My muscles are sore. How are your legs doing?'

With every step I took they summoned up painful memories of yesterday afternoon, and I launched into a clumsy apology.

'We should never have done that hike in one day,' he interrupted me. 'Even if we had gone there in one day and come back the next it would have been a nasty trek. If Rudy were still alive he'd give me a dressing down. Irresponsible. Rudy knew exactly how far he could go. But there's one thing we can be thankful for: if we'd come back a day later, we would never have made it through the valley. And that valley is the only way to get to the Río Moroco; I wonder how we would ever have made it back to Ucaima. Anyway, the best thing to do now is pack our gear.'

He pointed at the sky, which had been growing increasingly hazy since dawn. The fire must have climbed the hills by now, and was creeping north.

'Francisco says the river will protect his *conuco* from the fire, but I don't feel like waiting around here to see whether the flames will jump the water. The river isn't all that wide. This could become a catastrophe, it's been five months since the last rain, the trees are like tinder, the grass has turned to straw, there are forest fires right now in other parts of the Gran Sabana too. The last reports I heard on the shortwave said that part of the Amazon is on fire, and it's heading for the southernmost *tepuys*. We should get out of here.'

He waded into the stream, knelt down under the little waist-high waterfall, soaped his chest and squeezed the ticks out of the back of his neck. I took off my pants and counted forty bites on my thighs alone.

'Dab them with alcohol right away,' he warned me. 'Otherwise you'll be covered in sores in three days' time. First alcohol, then salve. And thank the Holy Virgin Mary that the *karapatos* weren't too fond of your balls.'

Our packs were much lighter when we set out for home. Olaf had left almost all his clothes at the *conuco*; I had given my shirts, T-shirt, socks and underpants to Victorino.

Francisco was sorry to see us go. 'Because of the dogs,' he said. 'Now we have no dogs again.'

Victorino walked with us to the Río Moroco; he was expecting his family.

Late in the morning we heard the regular splash of paddles in the water. A canoe appeared around a bend in the river; Victorino, who was lying in the shade of a tree, awoke, rubbed the sleep out of his eyes and nodded; these were, indeed, his relatives.

Victorino's wife, children and father-in-law were preparing to get out of the boat. Victorino gestured to them to remain seated. He gave no further explanation, he simply called out three or four words which Olaf translated for me.

'We must keep on walking.'

Victorino slid his machete into his belt, pressed the rifle against his chest and climbed into the canoe. He had given my clothes to Antonio; the only thing he'd kept for himself was the hammock. He was a proud man.

'When you go past Ucaima,' Olaf shouted after him, 'tell the boatsman to come and pick us up.'

Victorino stuck up his thumb. Then he turned around, sat down in the middle of the canoe and hunched over. His bent back was the last we saw of him.

José Castro showed up about halfway through the afternoon.

The water was lower than it had been on the way up. The prop kept hitting the rocks on the bottom; to keep the damage to the blades to a minimum, we went down the Moroco very slowly. The sky became an evening sky; the horizon faded; the smoke veiled the mountains.

Only when we turned up the broad Río Carrao did José use all twenty-five of the motor's horses. The bow wave splashed up high and sprayed into the boat.

Olaf turned around.

'Rudy couldn't swim. It's a miracle he never drowned. Whenever the boat would turn over in the rapids, he had to grab a paddle fast. One time a Venezuelan guide pushed him off the boat in the middle of the river. He had to dive in after him right away, Rudy was gasping for breath. The next day Rudy took the Venezuelan along in his Cessna when he went to Puerto Ordaz. He was going to pick up an American photographer who wanted to go out looking for a black panther, which is very rare. Once they were at cruising altitude, Rudy closed the throttle; the plane fell like a rock. 'So,' Rudy said to the Venezuelan, 'now you see how funny it is to scare the hell out of someone.' The Venezuelan pissed his pants, literally. Before they'd even landed, he'd handed in his resignation.'

That evening the sky was a glowing red; the fire was creeping across the savanna. It must have covered forty kilometres in a single day. The wind picked up, and I remembered what I'd heard about the bombardment of Rotterdam: that the flames had drawn in such enormous quantities of oxygen that, everywhere around the city, the wind came howling through.

The next day the fire had crossed the savanna, by evening it had reached the forest close to Ucaima. The camp itself was in no danger, the fire ate its way through the woods across the river, but the Río Carrao, which is at least two hundred metres across at Ucaima, formed a safe buffer. We could hear the wood crackle and hiss, however, and were overcome by a sense of doom.

After dinner we went to Rudy's round room down by the river, the room with the panoramic view. Not only the woods, but the entire sky as well seemed to be on fire. The white walls of the room were lit in a pinkish light. It was precisely as apocalyptic as Rudy had predicted in 1984, when Millicent Smeets-Muskus asked him how he saw the future. 'Black. Absolutely black.'

'He lost his grip on the area,' Olaf said. 'Every time a boat from Canaima came by here with twenty or thirty tourists on board, lined up neatly two by two and wearing those stupid orange life jackets prescribed by the Venezuelan government, Rudy would say: look, there goes another bus. The boats they took upriver kept getting bigger, with bigger motors all the time; they raced up the Río Carrao and the Río Churún in order to get to Angel Falls in a day and back. The louder the motors roared, the further the wild animals fled into the forest. And that in turn forced the Indian hunters to hack their way even further through the jungle. One day, one of those boats passed us on the Churún. Rudy stood up in the *curiare*, grabbed his rifle and yelled: "Oh, I'd just love to gun down a couple of tour operators."'

A little later that evening, Armando joined us. He looked exhausted; during our absence he had taken a group of parachutists to Angel Falls, Americans and Australians who had paid ten thousand dollars to make a thousand metre jump. The alcohol had flowed like water, to help them work up the nerve. Of course he had knocked back his share along with them, to forget his own worries. Sabine was blaming him for so much that he no longer knew exactly what she blamed him for most – the first divorce proceedings had already begun. He wouldn't be staying here much longer. He had assumed the daily management of the camp, but if the divorce went through he would have to go looking for another job. 'An impossible woman,' he sighed. 'Just as impossible as her father.'

Olaf agreed that you never knew exactly what was up with Rudy. If you wanted to make him swear, all you had to do was mention Holland, but the Dutch were the only people he trusted. The worst kind to him were the Venezuelans; still, he had traded in his Dutch passport for a Venezuelan one. He travelled far into Germany and Austria with films and documentation to lure nature-lovers to the Gran Sabana, but if one of his guests didn't appeal to him he would say: 'Here's your money back, now get lost.' He knew no compromise, was extreme in many ways, and could only get along with strongwilled people.

He was crazy about the Gerti who could cold-bloodedly shoot an anaconda through the head, he was crazy about the Gerti who had her picture taken with a pistol on her hip; he detested the Gerti who was constantly 'pinching pennies'. He was crazy about his daughters, until Lily went to make a new life for herself in the capital, until Sabine got involved with the first guide who came along, and until Gaby married a gnome who asked him:'What temperature does water freeze at?' One disillusionment could turn his love turn to hatred. The only thing that made up for that was his equally complicated love-hate relationship with himself.

Olaf summoned up memories of the Rudy he had met in 1988. Of course he hadn't completely gotten over Gerti's death yet, and it irritated him that he could no longer drive his body to the limit, but he still put in eighteen hour days if necessary. For a man who had never relaxed a day in his life, who had suffered from the worst tropical diseases, who had broken almost everything a person can break – an arm, a leg, a finger, a rib, who had even broken his back once in a fall on the north face of the Auyán Tepui – that was an incredible achievement. While installing a water tank, a cement trough fell on his foot; he was flown to Cíudad Bolívar, the surgeon on duty tried to repair his mashed ankle with pins. It took him a whole year to recover, but no matter how he exercised, he was never able to walk well again. But he still climbed the Auyán Tepui a few times.

When Olaf had come back to Ucaima in 1992, he found Rudy completely worn out. He weighed less than fifty kilos, was clearly ill, couldn't do much of anything anymore but hang over the table and look around with deep, sad eyes. He only perked up when Lupé would come and sit down beside him on the couch. He would put his arm around her, and his daughters would walk out of the dining room. That badgering – or was it misplaced anxiety? – infuriated him, and when he became angry he became unreasonable. 'I'll throw them out so fast it will make their heads spin!' he shouted to Olaf, who looked the other way in embarrassment. When Gaby left, at last, he asked Olaf to take over the camp from him. Olaf wouldn't consider it for a moment.

'Man,' he had shouted at Rudy, 'life in the wide-open spaces is over. You belong to a different era. If you started now, you'd never get Ucaima going; the Venezuelans would block you every step of the way.'

The Venezuelan inspectors stepped back in deference for trigger-happy Rudy, but also out of respect for what he had built on his own, without any help. Olaf, on the other hand, they would see as just another foreigner moving in on the tastiest pieces of the Venezuelan pie. He would have to negotiate for days, for weeks, with civil servants who wanted their palms greased for every little thing, and who rarely kept their promises. He didn't feel like putting energy into that. Rudy saw his refusal as added proof that he was gradually becoming a hermit living in his own dreams.

He felt worse all the time. A year went by. Then he asked Lily to come back, and soon afterwards Sabine as well, which implied that Olaf would have to leave.

The cancer was in his lungs, his stomach, his knees. In the end, he came down with the same thing that had killed his wife – a brain tumor. Was it coincidence, or had they both breathed in too much asbestos dust? During the last big renovation of the camp, both Rudy and Gerti had spent weeks sawing asbestos roofing material, not knowing how carcinogenic it was. The diet of sardines and rice on which they had often lived for weeks must have undermined their health as well. And Rudy had always lived with the assumption that the air he breathed was so clean that the two packs of cigarettes he smoked each day, and the pipes he lit up between times, could have no ill effects on him.

Finally, he was too ill to stay at the camp. In Carácas they removed his right lung. He had radiation treatment. He also underwent a new kind of chemotherapy, which cost him ten thousand dollars. He fought, because that was what he'd always done best: fight, even when no one gave him a ghost of a chance.

Lupé went with him to Carácas. She took care of him for months. His hair fell out, whole clumps of it, and when he stood in front of the mirror he would sigh: 'Look at me, Lupé, I'm starting to look like Mahatma Gandhi, a ninety-year-old looks better than I do.' When he felt the end approaching, he flew back to the Gran Sabana. He wanted to die at Ucaima.

His birthday, on December 7th, ended in a fight. Once again his daughters demanded that Lupé leave. He was too weak to react, and Lupé packed her bags. She got a job as a receptionist at the Avensa Hotel in Canaima.

When I arrived in Canaima for the second time, in 1998, she was still working there. I called and made an appointment with her, but the day before we were to meet she quit her job, flew to Carácas, and from Carácas to Lima: this finally gave her something in common with the Truffino girls – she, too, preferred to remain silent.

Once Lupé had left the camp, the girls no longer troubled themselves about their father, and went back to Carácas and Puerto Ordaz. During the final weeks of his life there was no one Rudy could count on for help. The only one who ever checked on him was Armando.

He could no longer talk, he could no longer defecate. He would stumble out onto the lawn in front of his house, pull down his pants, squat, growl and moan like an animal in distress. His face contorted with pain, he then went back to his hammock and underlined the passages in *The General in his Labyrinth* that expressed Simon Bolivar's bitterness and desolation. Or he listened to a distant cry and wondered what kind of bird it was. No name came up in his mind, not in Spanish, not in the language of his youth. He leafed through his photo album and stopped for a long time at the photo of the sleek wooden dinghy in which he had sailed as a boy on the Kaag and the lakes around Nieuwkoop. He took the picture of Els in his hands and searched blearily for her bright eyes. He tried to sit up, and fell back exhausted in the hammock. Sometimes Armando would pick him up, carry him to the bar and set him on a stool. He would remain sitting there for half an hour, then Armando would carry him back to his house.

He spent the Christmas holidays alone; Armando had gone to celebrate them with his two children in the capital. There was no one with him at New Year's either; Armando was in Canaima. The last few hours of his life, Truffino looked in vain for a familiar face; the only one who kept him company was his dog.

A few hours after he died, Olaf received a call from Gaby. He was on Margarita at the time. One day later he arrived at Ucaima. By then, the other daughters had flown in as well. They asked the authorities for permission to bury Rudy at the edge of his camp, organized a brief ceremony, and placed a simple headstone on his grave. Olaf couldn't remember whether any of the twelve people at the funeral had wept.

Just before midnight, the fire reached the Sapo falls. There, before getting to Canaima, it stopped.

The next morning we took the canoe east, across the charred savannas. The smoke gradually floated away, and everywhere on the plain we saw Indians walking, looking for fertile plots of land.

At dusk we listened to the soft, high voice of Simon Diaz. Armando hummed along with the songs, which sang of the plains, the coasts, the savannas and the mesas of Venezuela. I saw myself as the old Truffino, shuffling amid the furniture I had built myself, with brittle cheeks, dull eyes, searching for words in the language I had learned as a child, and unable to utter a syllable. Olaf took off his glasses, kneaded the bridge of his nose between thumb and forefinger, and asked: 'So when are we going up there?'

The next day we made our first concrete plans for a long trip over the Auyán Tepui and we plotted a route that would take us past towers of rock and cliffs to a chasm that Rudy Truffino, on the maps he had drawn himself, had given a name that only he could have come up with. We were going to look for the Lonely Passage.

A word of thanks

This book was made possible with the help of Olaf Hendriksz, and of Emile Brugman, Marco Delli Carpini, José Castro, Peter-Paul Chaudron, Marta Gomez, Josef Gregori, Els ten Houte de Lange, Juan Jiménez, Derk Lanting, Victorino Manrique, Antonio Monte, Florencia Monte, Francisco Monte de Oca, Otilia Monte, Francisco Pacheco, Armando Tovar, Arabella van Tienhoven van de Bogaard, Joost Reintjes, the Dutch Embassy in Carácas, Millicent Smeets-Muskus, Han Truffino, Ingrid Truffino, Lily Truffino de Serrano and Gaby Truffino de Jiménez.

Thanks also to the Dutch *Fonds voor de Letteren*, from whom I received a travel grant that allowed me to visit the Gran Sabana for the second time.

The definitive version of *Jungle Rudy* was written at Schloss Wiepersdorf, in the Brandenburg woods, where I stayed for three months at the invitation of the *German Stiftung Kulturfonds*.

251

List of sources quoted and consulted

Armellada, R.P. Cesareo de *Grammatica y Diccionario de la Lengua Pemón*, Caracas, 1943

———, *Tauron Ponton Cuentos y Legendas de los Indios Pemóns*, Caracas, 1964

———, *Pemonton Taremuru: Invocaciones Magicas de los Indios Pemón*, Caracas,1972

Bates, Henry Walter *The Naturalist on the River Amazon: A Record of Adventures, Habits of Animals, Sketches of Brazilian and Indian Life, and Aspects of Nature under the Equator, during Eleven Years of Travel*, 2 parts, London, 1863

Bock, Ron. F. *Bezuidenhout-Toen*, Rotterdam, 1970

Boom, B. van der *Den Haag in dc Tweede Wereldoorlog*, The Hague, 1995

Booth, Martin *The Doctor, the Detective and Arthur Conan Doyle: A Biography of Arthur Conan Doyle*, London, 1997

Brewer-Cariás, Charles *La Vegetación del Mundo Perdido*, Carácas, 1978

Carpentier, Alejo *Los pasos perdidos*, Mexico D.E, 1953

Dennison, L.R. *Devil Mountain*, New York, 1942

Doyle, Sir Arthur Conan *The Lost World*, London, 1912

———, *Memories and Adventures,* Londen, 1924

Dunsterville, Galfrid C.K. *Las Orquideas de Venezuela*, Carácas,1987

————, 'Auyantepui', *Boletin de la Sociedad Venezolana de Ciencias Naturales*, September 1965, no. 109, Carácas

————, '*Auyantepui Again*, 1964, unpublished account of the expedition with R. J. M. Truffino

Dunsterville, G.C.K, and Garay, Leslie A. *Venezuelan Orchids*, 6 parts, London, 1966

Ferguson, James *Venezuela*, Amsterdam, The Hague, 1994

Gallegos, Romulo *Canaima*, Carácas, 1935

Garcia Marquez, Gabriel *El general en su laberinto*, Mexico, 1989

George, Uwe *Inselen in der Zeit. Venezuela-Expeditionen zu den letzten weissen Flecken der Erde*, Hamburg, 1988

————, 'Venezuela's Islands in Time', *National Geographic*, Vol. 175, no. 5, May 1989

————, 'Auf der Suche nach dem Ungeheuer', *Geo*, no. 12, 1990

————, 'Durch die Wüste lebt der Regenwald', *Geo*, no. 3, 1995

Gheerbrant, Alain *Orenoque-Amazone, 1948-1950*, Paris 1952, republished 1992

Goslinga, Cornelis Ch. *De Nederlanders in Venezuela*. Bilingual edition, *Los holandeses en Venezuela*, Carácas, 1992

Helman, Albert *Kroniek van Eldorado*. Book 1: Folteraars over en weer. Book 2: Gefolterden zonder verweer, Amsterdam, 1983. Revised and expanded edition, Amsterdam, 1995

Humboldt, A. von *Voyages aux Regions Equinoxiales du Nouveau Continent*, 13 vol. Paris, 1816–1831

————, *Personal Narrative of Travels to the Equinoctial Regions of the New Continent, during the years 1799-1804*, by Alexander de Humboldt and Aimé Bonpland, 7 vol. London 1814–1829

————, *Südamerikanische Reise. Ideen iiber Ansichten der Natur*, Berlin, 1943

Huppertz, J. (ed) *Geister am Roraima. Indianer Mythen, Sagen und Marchen aus Guayana*, Kassel, 1956

Koch-Grunberg, Theodor *Zwei Jahre unter den Indianen*, 2 vol., Berlin, 1910

———, *Indianer Märchen aus Südamerika*, Jena, 1920

———, *Vom Roraima zum Orinoco: Ergebnisse einer Reise im Nordbrasilien und Venezuela in den Jahren 1911-13*, 3 vol., Berlin, 1929

Korthals Altes, A. *Luchtgevaar, luchtaanvallen op Nederland 1940-1945*, Amsterdam, 1984

Lacey, Robert *Sir Walter Raleigh*, London, 1974

Leeuwen, Boeli van *De rots der struikeling*, Amsterdam, 1960

Lemm, Robert *Eldorado*, Amsterdam, 1996

Levi-Strauss, Claude *Tristes tropiques*, Paris, 1955

Lizot, Jacques *La Cercle des Feux, Faits en dits indiens Yanomami*, Paris, 1976

———, *El Circulo de los Fuegos, Vida y costumbres de los indios Yanomami*, Carácas, 1978

McIntyre, Loren 'Humboldt's Way', *National Geographic*, vol. 168, no. 3, September 1985

Melham, Tom 'Lost World of the Tepuis', in the National Geographic Society special edition *Beyond the Horizon*, 1992

Mills, Dorothy *The Country of the Orinoco*, London , 1931

Moron, Guillermo *A History of Venezuela*, London, 1964

O'Hanlon, Redmond *In Trouble Again*, London, 1988

———, *Tussen Orinoco en Amazon*, Amsterdam, 1988

Oliva-Esteva, Francisco, and Steyermark, Julian A. *Bromeliaceaes of Venezuela*, Carácas, 1987

Plotkin, Mark J. *In de leer bij de sjamanen. Een botanicus op zoek naar nieuwe medicijnen in het Amazone regenwoud*, Rijswijk, 1995

Ralegh (Raleigh), W. *The Discoverie of the Large, Rich and Bewtiful Empyre of Gviana*, London, 1596

Robertson, Ruth *Churún Merú: The Tallest Angel*, Pennsylvania, 1977

Röhl, Eduardo *Fauna descriptica de Venezuela*, Carácas, 1962

Rouse, Irving, and Cruxent, Jose M. *Venezuela Archaeology*, New Haven, 1963

Schama, Simon *Landschap en herrinering*, Amsterdam, 1995

Schauensee, Rodolphe Meyer de, and Phelps Jr., William H. *A Guide to the Birds of Venezuela*, Princeton, 1978

Schomburgk, M.R. *Reisen in Britisch-Guiana in den Jahren 1840-1844*, 3 vol., Leipzig, 1847-1848

Schomburgk, O.H. *Robert Hermann Schomburgk's Travels in Guiana and on the Orinoco during the years 1835-1839, according to his reports and communications to the Geographical Society of London*, Georgetown B.G., 1931

Schomburgk, R.H. *A Description of British Guiana*, London, 1840

———, *Richard Schomburgk's Travels in British Guiana 1840-1844*, Georgetown B.G., 1922

Schubert, C. and Huber, 0. *The Gran Sabana: Panorama of a Region*, Carácas, 1990

Smeets-Muskus, Millicent *Een Hagenaar in het oerwoud*, unpublished interview, 1984

Spruce, Richard *Notes of a Botanist on the Amazon and Andes, being records of travel on the Amazon and its tributaries, the Trombetas, Rio Negro, Uapés, Casiquiari, Pacimoni, Huallaga, and Pastasa; as also to the cataracts of the Orinoco, along the Eastern side of the Andes of Peru and Ecuador, and the shores of the Pacific, during the years 1849-1864*, 2 vol. London, 1908

Steyermark, J.A. 'Expedition to the Lost World', *Missouri Botanical Garden Bulletin*, 1986

Steyermark, Julian A., Berry, Paul E., Holst, Bruce K. *Flora of the Venezuelan Guayana*, Missouri, 1995, vol. 1 and 2

Stichting 3 maart 1945-1995 *Van Haagsche Bosch tot Haagse Poort*, The Hague, 1995

Tate, G.H.H. 'Auyantepui: Notes on the Phelps Venezuelan Expedition', *Geographical Review* 28, New York, 1938

Thomas, D.J. 'Order Without Government: The Society of the Pemon Indians of Venezuela', *Illinois Studies in Anthropology*, no. 13, Urbana, 1982

Thoreau, Henry David *Journal*, vol. 1, Princeton, 1981

Thurn, Everard F. *In Among the Indians of Guiana, being sketches chiefly anthropologic from the interior of British Guiana*, London, 1883

Vareschi, Volkmar *Flora de Venezuela*, Carácas, 1958

Wallace, Alfred R. A *Narrative of Travels on the Amazon and Rio Negro, with an account of the Native Tribes, and Observations on the Climate, Geology and Natural History of the Amazon Valley*, London, 1853

Weidmann, Karl, Perez Vila, Manuel, Huber, Otto *La Gran Sabana*, Carácas, 1986

Whitehead, Neil L. *Lord of the Tiger Spirit, A History of the Caribs in Colonial Venezuela and Guyana 1498-1820*, Dordrecht, 1988